ALSO BY UCADIA

    Lebor Clann Glas

    Five Worlds

    De Dea Magisterium

    Waiata

    Tara

Yapa

**OFFICIAL ENGLISH
FIRST EDITION**

BY

UCADIA

Ucadia Books Company

Yapa. Official English First Edition. Copyright © 2012-2020 UCADIA. All Rights reserved in Trust.

No part of this book may be reproduced, or stored in a retrieval system, or transmitted in any form or by any means electronic, mechanical, photocopying, recording or otherwise, without the express and authentic written permission of the Publisher.

The Publisher disclaims any liability and shall be indemnified and held harmless from any demands, loss, liability, claims or expenses made by any party due or arising out of or in connection with any differences between previous non-official English drafts and this Official English First Edition.

A party that threatens, makes or enacts any demand or action, against this publication or the Publisher hereby acknowledge they have read this disclaimer and agree with this binding legal agreement and irrevocably consent to Ucadia and its competent forums as being the original and primary Jurisdiction for resolving any such issue of fact and law.

Published by Ucadia Books Company, a Delaware stock corporation (File Number 6779670) 901 N Market St #705 Wilmington Delaware 19801. First edition.

UCADIA® is a US Registered Trademark in trust under Guardians and Trustees Company protected under international law and the laws of the United States.

ISBN 978-1-64419-010-4

Preface

We are the dancing wind through the grasses and trees. We are the summer rains and swirling mists of steam rising from the rocks. We are the echoes of the nesting birds at dawn and the humming of the insects at dusk.

We are the first spirits, the first forms and the first ancestors of country. We are the first memories and all memories of life and change of country. We are all born of country and all spirit of country, whether black or white, new or old, male or female. We are all and more than the land called by the southern spirit name of Australia.

Listen then to our words of true law of country, of first law of peoples called Yapa. A pure heart will know and a clear mind will see. A poisoned heart will feel nothing and a clouded mind be blind to truth.

Nothing created can be uncreated. Nothing born of spirit can be unmade. Yet all form of spirit changes as country changes. Once this land was under great ice as the end of the world, when no animals or people did walk. Once these lands were great inland seas where only fish swam. Once these lands were lush forests and the home of giant spirit animals.

All changes but truth and memory of the first ancestors and the first spirits. Truth, knowledge and memory be hard teachers, but necessary. Those who still respect the nature of right initiation know of such pain, but also of the healing of true knowledge. The knowledge of far sight that can see the truth that all is spirit and the difference. The knowledge of life and meaning and the power of stillness of mind. The knowledge of the people and the law that flows through the living bodies of all borne to country, no matter if they be connected by blood or skin or ancestor – all are connected to first nations by the true spirit.

People did not begin to lose unity to us upon the arrival of strange cultures or even disease. The pain of truth is witness in our divided languages; and our divided stories; and our divided memory of knowledge. Other peoples did not do this to the first peoples of country. We say to you that many who claim to speak for country and our spirit will reject Yapa and even our words. That will stand as an I and speak and act as an I and that only they speak as we.

It is the laws of men and women not first spirit that formed the boundary of circle that prevented much memory and knowledge from communication except to the right initiated. So it is the laws of men and women, however wise for many generations, that did condemn such forgetfulness so men and women have no knowledge of family, or country, or spirit.

The painful truth be that they are hollow not for the injury caused by others but the intentional injury and ignorance against the spirit within them, that the illness of I causes to many.

We have never abandoned first people of country. We cannot be taken from country for we are all. Only those choose to live with hearts closed, and eyes blind and ears blocked cannot understand this. The source of spirit has always come to you, sung, spoken with you, nurtured you. Remember then, feel then, that you have always heard us and seen us before! Awaken!

Wake up, all our people, a new dawn is breaking. Country is waking to a bright new day when none forget us, no limitation may defeat us, nor colour divide us. Obsess upon the past no more, on the years and failings behind you. The unending love and knowledge revealed to you shall replace all of it.

When a true initiate of country embraces Yapa, there be no need to curse or betray the trust of others. So long have you wait till hate and doubt seemed to consume you. No more! Now light guides you, there can be no doubt. No goal of unity between the first peoples and all born to country cannot be denied.

All paths and song lines be restored and opened. This be the time of healing and the new Dream Time. Remember who have spoken these words before and who have always guided you and remember who you are and we are.

For those that are yet to come, sing of joy to all our brothers and sisters, aunties and uncles and cousins. Country welcomes and loves you.

First Australian Law

The Indigenous Nations of Australia (Aboriginal Australians) are the oldest surviving civilized cultures and longest permanent owners and occupiers of land in human history. The Original Australian nations are the only surviving Mesolithic Culture (older than 15,000 years). The Indigenous Nations of Australia are also the oldest surviving Palaeolithic Culture (older than 40,000 years).

Of all forms of original law and human civilisation, the original law and first culture of Australia is fundamental to humanity itself. The First Law of the First Peoples of the First Nations of Australia is the oldest surviving law of humanity. The Law of the first peoples of Australia is their culture and Indigenous culture is one with the law.

The First Law of the First Peoples of the First Nations of Australia is able to provide a context to the origin and significance of all human law and civilisation. The oldest authentic surviving law of humanity is able to conclusively demonstrate that certain principles are and have always been present in any functional system of law and society.

Knowledge of family and tribe, both in terms of names, relations and notable traits has always been at the heart of learning, memory, law and society. The sheer discipline of learning such complex mosaics and relations gave our ancestors the capacity to then learn and remember other complex arrangements, such as plants, animals and signs of seasons and change.

Knowledge of ritual, especially in terms of language, movements and sequence has always been a central element of binding people of all cultures and history. Respect for knowledge, memory of knowledge right initiation in order to be granted the right to learn the most important knowledge has also been a fundamental role of preserving culture and rule of law.

Yet similar to many other Paleolithic and Mesolithic cultures long since extinct, Indigenous Australian Law historically strictly prevented (until now) such knowledge from being transmitted to others "outside the circle" of the initiated. This has presented an impenetrable moral dilemma. Sadly the effects of modern society has severely damaged this tradition. Furthermore, such protections of the law have been continuously misused to deny the existence or completeness of Aboriginal Australian law.

Yapa is an inspired and divine work, revealed by the spirits of the land known as Australia. No laws were broken in the writing of Yapa.

Contents

The First Age of Spirit

Book 1	The Beginning..	1
Book 2	The Dreaming...	11
Book 3	The Spirits..	17
Book 4	The Star People...	23
Book 5	The First Law...	29

The Second Age of Flesh

Book 6	The First Great Tribulation...	33
Book 7	The Second Law..	41
Book 8	The Wars...	57

The Third Age of Mind

Book 9	The Second Great Tribulation...	61
Book 10	The Third Law..	69
Book 11	One Law One People One Country...................................	87

To each and every child borne upon the land known as Australia, since the beginning of time.

Rise up, you are the sun, you are the earth, you are the dance of life.

Unknown Aboriginal Elder

The First Age of Spirit
Book 1
The Beginning

C. 1 - The Beginning

Before one speaks, 2 as it has always been custom, 3 for all law to be justice it must be spoken; 4 by One whom possesses Right to speak, 5 and by One whom carries Right spirit of knowledge, 6 and One whom demonstrates Respect of right ceremony. 7 All words and language are sacred. 8 All language when assembled in right ceremony and right spirit, 9 be the most precious gift of all. 10 Without right language, there is no life, 11 only existence. 12 Without right language, 13 there be no right ceremony. 14 Without right ceremony and spirit, 15 there be no country. 16 Since the Dreaming, there has been only One Law; 17 One Law from beginning of Creation. 18 While many peoples have come and gone; 19 law has never died or left the land. 20 Honour the Law. Honour Yapa and you honour all peoples. 21 This is why most ancient of ancestors sung (in ceremony): 22 *"One Law, One Language, One Custom."*

C. 2 - The Right

1 Who is worthy to hear wisdom of the ancestors? 2 Who is honourable to hear and partake in law? 3 Not just one family, but all tribes. 4 Not just people of the dreaming, but all peoples. 5 When we speak of ancestors, 6 we speak of ancestors of creation and all people. 7 Spirit people that created all existence; 8 spirit people that created the star people; 9 spirit people that created this world; 10 the way it was from the beginning. 11 No one be above the law. 12 All are the same under the law. 13 If such rule does not exist, 14 no rule of law exists. 15 This first law has always been most sacred. 16 This is why for generation to generation, 17 from before the time of our great ancestors, 18 before even the time of the great animals, 19 only those who knew the right Way, 20 were permitted to hear, 21 and were allowed to see. 22 If a man or woman did not show respect for the elders, 23 the stories were forbidden to be spoken. 24 If a man or woman behaved as a child, 25 they be treated as a child. 26 Never to hear the words of the Ancestors; 27 never to be shown right ceremony. 28 Only those who knew the Right Way. 29 But now we have come to the Third Age, 30 and The Age of the Mind. 31 The Spirit Ancestors call us to be teachers: 32 to show the right Way; 33 to teach the right knowledge; 34 to explain right ceremony; 35 to restore knowledge of the Law, 36 even when those do not honour the Right Way. 37 To forgive them, 38 even when they

disrespect sacred sanctuary. 39 To forgive them and teach them. 40 To write down in symbols what has always been most sacred; 41 what has been most secret, 42 so all may know. 43 As the ancient song of wisdom of the ancients reminds us: 44 *"Nothing is gone, Everything Changes"*

C. 3 - The Way to See and Hear

1 Before you hear our story, 2 before you hear your story, 3 or the writing of the language, 4 of the country of our ancestors, 5 and the country of your ancestors, 6 or the name of a spirit or ancestor, 7 or their skin or an animal, or a song, 8 or the way of ceremony and dignity, 9 or the way of family and tribe, 10 you must be able to see properly, 11 you must be able to hear properly. 12 Above all things, you must be able to think properly. 13 A man who cannot see, is blind even with eyes. 14 A woman who cannot hear is deaf even with ears. 15 A mind that is full of precondition and ideas, 16 yet without proper initiation, 17 cannot think the proper way of law, 18 nor the ways taught by the ancestors. 19 Because you have been educated to read, 20 does not mean you are not blind. 21 To truly see, you must feel your feet on the ground, 22 smell the air, feel the sun on your skin. 23 If you think you can hear because there is no noise, 24 then you cannot. 25 To hear, you must hear your heartbeat, 26 hear and feel the sound of the raindrops on earth, 27 the shifting of sand even when ants make their nest. 28 If you cannot properly see or hear, 29 then you will not see the Right Path. 30 A man or woman without right initiation, 31 cannot see what is in front of him. 32 This is why the ancients sung: 33 *"Cover eyes (to) see, block ears (to) hear."*

C. 4 - The Required Knowledge

1 It be the law from the First Age, 2 to be initiated as a man or women, 3 a boy or girl must know: 4 the count and name of their family; 5 the count and name of their ancestors. 6 This be the knowledge of themselves; 7 this be the knowledge of respect; 8 this be the first path of knowledge. 9 A boy or girl who disowns family is lost. 10 A boy or girl who disrespects the memory of ancestors, 11 is alone in spirit and easy prey. 12 A boy or girl who refuses to learn, 13 is an empty space. 14 To respect family, 15 to count and name family generations, 16 is the path to all knowledge. 17 From the count and naming of family generations, 18 comes count and naming of species. 19 From the count and naming of species, 20 comes the count, naming and preparation of food. 21 From the count and naming of species, 22 and from the count and preparation of food, 23 comes naming of all country. 24 From the count and naming of all country, 25 comes name and count of days and seasons. 26 From the count and name of days and seasons, 27 comes count and name of moons and years. 28 From the count and name of moons and years, 29 comes count and name of constellations. 30 From the count and name of all knowledge, 31 comes count and name of Law. 32 From the count and name of Law comes all Culture and Identity, 33 as Culture and Identity is nothing if not founded on

the true origin of Law. 34 This is why first ancestors spoke: 35 *"First (is) family, second (is) family, all (is) family."*

C. 5 - The Count and Name of Generations

1 Of all the knowledge one must learn, 2 the first and last is family. 3 Father we call "father"; 4 mother we call "mother"; 5 sister from the same mother or father we call "sister"; 6 and women of the same skin name and moiety we call "sister"; 7 brother from the same mother or father we call "brother"; 8 and men from the same skin name and moiety we call "brother"; 9 and brother of our father or mother we call "uncle"; 10 and older men of the same moiety as teachers we call "uncle"; 11 and sister of our father or mother we call "aunty"; 12 and older women of the same moiety as teachers we call "aunty"; 13 our son we call "boy" or "son"; 14 and the son of our brothers or sisters we call "boy" or "nephew"; 15 our daughter we call "girl" or "daughter"; 16 and the daughter of our brothers or sisters we call "girl" or "niece"; 17 our grandson we call "boy" or "son"; 18 and the grandson of our brothers or sisters we call "boy" or "grandnephew"; 19 our granddaughter we call "girl" or "granddaughter"; 20 and the granddaughter of our brothers or sisters we call "girl" or "grand niece"; 21 our grandfather we call "grandfather" or "elder"; 22 and grandfathers of the same moiety we call "grandfather" or "elder"; 23 our grandmother we call "grandmother" or "lady"; 24 and grandmothers of the same moiety we call "grandmother" or "lady"; 25 and all those who have lived and died from the tribe we call "ancestors"; 26 and all sisters that have died within a year we do not speak their name; 27 and all brothers that have died within a year we do not speak their name; 28 and all girls, daughters or nieces that have died, we do not speak their name for three years; 29 and all boys, sons or nephews that have died, we do not speak their name for three years; 30 and all mothers, aunties and ladies that have died, we do not speak their name for five years; 31 and all fathers, uncles and elders that have died, we do not speak their name for five years; 32 we call our father ancestor our "father" or "father ancestor" and all boys, sons, nephews, fathers, uncles and elders of our father ancestor we call first ancestors and their relation; 33 we call our mother ancestor our "mother" or "mother ancestor" and all girls, daughters, nieces, mothers, aunties and ladies of our mother ancestor we call first ancestors and their relation; 34 we call our grandfather ancestor our "grandfather" or "first grandfather ancestor" and all boys, sons, nephews, fathers, uncles and elders of our first grandfather ancestor we call second ancestors and their relation; 35 we call our grandmother ancestor our "grandmother" or "first grandmother ancestor" and all girls, daughters, nieces, mothers, aunties and ladies of our first grandmother ancestor we call second ancestors and their relation; 36 we call our great grandfather ancestor our "second grandfather ancestor" and all boys, sons, nephews, fathers, uncles and elders of our second grandfather ancestor we call third ancestors and their relation; 37 we call

our great grandmother ancestor our "second grandmother ancestor" and all girls, daughters, nieces, mothers, aunties and ladies of our second grandmother ancestor we call third ancestors and their relation; 38 we call our great great grandfather ancestor our "third grandfather ancestor" and all boys, sons, nephews, fathers, uncles and elders of our third grandfather ancestor we call fourth ancestors and their relation; 39 we call our great great grandmother ancestor our "third grandmother ancestor" and all girls, daughters, nieces, mothers, aunties and ladies of our third grandmother ancestor we call fourth ancestors and their relation; 40 we call our great great great grandfather ancestor our "fourth grandfather ancestor" and all boys, sons, nephews, fathers, uncles and elders of our fourth grandfather ancestor we call fifth ancestors and their relation; 41 we call our great great great grandmother ancestor our "fourth grandmother ancestor" and all girls, daughters, nieces, mothers, aunties and ladies of our fourth grandmother ancestor we call fifth ancestors and their relation; 42 our tribe of a different moiety we call "cousins" or "tribe"; 43 and members of the same skin name but from a different tribe we call "cousins" or "family"; 44 and members who share a common ancestor back to our one hundredth grandfather or grandmother ancestor we call "family". 45 A man or woman who cannot remember their ancestors, 46 cannot represent moiety or tribe. 47 Only men and women that honour family may represent family. 48 Only men and women that honour moiety may represent moiety. 49 Only men and women that keep alive the memory of ancestors, 50 may speak for ancestors and tribe. 51 As the ancient song of law tells us: 52 *"(Remember) family, (honour) ancestors, (honour) skin."*

C. 6 - The Count and Name of Species

1 To name and count the species of every animal and plant: 2 all animals that swim, that walk, that crawl, that jump and fly; 3 all two legged and four legged animals; 4 all species of plant, of grasses and tree; 5 this be the second path of knowledge. 6 First, one must learn and remember the count and name of family. 7 A boy or girl who do not learn family, 8 cannot learn the count and name of species. 9 They will say kangaroo, but they will not know kangaroo dreaming. 10 They will say snake, but they will not know snake dreaming. 11 They will say crocodile or emu, but they will not know crocodile or emu dreaming. 12 A boy or girl who first learns family, 13 can learn all manner of knowledge, 14 and can learn the count of name of species. 15 This is why first is family and last is family. 16 When a boy or girl can speak properly of first knowledge, 17 they are ready to learn second knowledge. 18 What be second knowledge? 19 It is the wisdom and knowledge of ancestors about species: 20 it is shape and look of every plant and animal, 21 and how it got its shape and look; 22 it is name of every plant and animal, 23 and how it got its name; 24 it is the spirit of plant and animal, 25 and how the spirit came to be inside that plant or animal; 26 it is family of every plant and animal, 27

and knowledge of its family; 28 it is how every animal moves and every plant grows, 29 and where it lives and what it does; 30 it is the origin of the species as a totem and skin name. 31 It is the respect of every species as custodians of country. 32 It is the ancient ceremony of skin and totem: 33 *"(animal/plant) spirit is me; we are (animal/plant) spirit."*

C. 7 - The Count and Name of Foods

1 To name and count and prepare Right Food: 2 before one hunts animals; 3 before one picks fruits or nuts or grasses; 4 before one opens the nests of insects; 5 one must know lawful food from forbidden and taboo food; 6 one must know good food from bad or poison food. 7 This is called the third path of knowledge. 8 A boy or girl who do not know the name and count of species, 9 will mistake bad fruits for good fruits; 10 will waste spear and stick chasing animal the wrong way; 11 will scatter the animals with their noise; 12 will cook wrong and make themselves sick; 13 will break the law in eating forbidden and taboo food. 14 Before one count and name and know the preparation of right food, 15 one must have second knowledge of species of all animals and plants. 16 Before one count and name species and plants, 17 one must have first knowledge of moiety, family and generations. 18 This is why we call the count and name of food the third path of knowledge. 19 What be third knowledge? 20 It is the wisdom and knowledge and law of ancestors about food: 21 it is the respect of every living animal and plant, 22 that allows its spirit to become one with the people for food. 23 To never hunt, except for food and supplies; 24 to never harvest or burn plants and grasses and trees, except at the right time; 25 to never pick fruit too early, or too late after the birds and bats spoil it; 26 to never be greedy with food or to over hunt or over burn; 27 to avoid killing pregnant animals because this will cause them to die out; 28 to take care of healing plants and never cause them to die from damage or over use; 29 to avoid torturing animals, because this causes the transfer of negative spirit; 30 to honour custom in the right preparation of right food; 31 to stay away from foods that cause narcotic effects, except in proper ceremony; 32 as the ancient and wisest ancestor women sung: 33 *"Right Food Live; Wrong Food Die."*

C. 8 - The Count and Name of Country

1 Only one who is a true custodian of country, 2 may count and name and speak of country. 3 It be Law from the First Age, 4 only men and women properly initiated into sacred office, 5 through proper ceremony be true custodians of country. 6 A man or woman not a proper custodian, 7 cannot speak for country. 8 Such a man or woman is an imposter. 9 Only men and women who respect what is sacred, 10 may speak of sacred things. 11 Sanctuary of country is most important and must not be violated. 12 The sacredness of sanctuary is the sacred of all holy places. 13 A people who respect nothing of sacredness, 14 have no culture or law. 15 A People who defile sanctuary, 16 curse their

own spirit and set themselves alone. 17 A man or woman who deliberately damage sanctuary, 18 can never be a custodian of land or country. 19 Before one be initiated as custodian of country, 20 one must know all of country: 21 every rock, every gully, every tree, every path; 22 every stream, every waterhole and song line; 23 every location of sacred sanctuary and temple; 24 every animal that swims, that walks, that crawls, that jumps and flys in country; 25 every species of plant, of grasses and tree in country; 26 every good food and every bad food of country; 27 every right food and every taboo food and drug of country. 28 To know the meeting places of family; 29 to know the ancient camp sites of tribe; 30 to know where one may walk and where one is forbidden to travel. 31 This is why we call the count and name of country the fourth knowledge. 32 A man or woman who does not know third knowledge, of food cannot learn country. 33 A man or woman who does not know second knowledge of species cannot learn country. 34 A man or woman who does not know first knowledge of moiety, family and generations cannot learn country. 35 When one knows country, one learns dreaming of country. 36 One acquires knowledge through ceremony to see country. 37 Not just see all that can be seen, but all that is not seen, 38 all spirit and disturbance of spirit. 39 When one learns country, one can see the tracks of spirit in country, 40 long after the fellow or animal has gone. 41 When one learns country, one can sense the changes coming, 42 well before the storm or winds rise up. 43 This is why the ancient elders sung: 44 *"(I) See you; (I) See you; (I) See you."*

C. 9 - The Count and Name of Days and Seasons

1 The cycle of seasons of wet; 2 the cycle of seasons of no water; 3 this be by law the knowledge of ceremony men and women; 4 initiated to office of country; 5 who speak to the ancestors and land, 6 and protect the tribe and all the animals and plants. 7 This be the fifth knowledge. 8 To know by day and season the coming change. 9 The change of drought to flood; 10 the change of heat to cold; 11 the change of calm to storm. 12 The initiated man or woman listens to country, 13 and listens to the animals and insects of country, 14 and listens to the plants and grasses of country. 15 The animals and insects speak change before it comes. 16 The plants and grasses tell of change before it arrives. 17 Even the rocks and waters give certain warnings and signs of season. 18 One cannot be an elder custodian of country, 19 if one does not count the days of seasons. 20 So the ancient elders of country, sung: 21 *"wattle (grow), bird (sing); good (country), dry (country)."*

C. 10 - The Count and Name of Moons and Years

1 The moon be our guardian, 2 and Great spirit. 3 The moon lights the land, 4 and reveals the song lines. 5 He tells us the path and the way. 6 He reminds us of the great stories, 7 of life, of death and return. 8 He teaches us to hunt in darkness; 9 he shows us to hunt in great light; 10 he comforts the ill and sick; 11 he accompanies the

ancestors; 12 he dances with us in ceremony; 13 he laughs with us at camp; 14 he visits each of the great constellations; 15 he celebrates a new born of the family; 16 he comforts us in our sorrow; 17 he reveals the truth; 18 he never lies; 19 he is a great guardian of dreaming. 20 To count the arrival of moon by full face, 21 is to count a cycle. 22 There be two hundred and thirty five cycle of the moon, 23 to nineteen cycles of seasons as one Generation, 24 and six thousand nine hundred and forty days. 25 This be the sixth knowledge, 26 and the knowledge of elders of ceremony. 27 This is why the ancients sung: 28 *"Honour (us) Moon; Reveal (to us) Moon."*

C. 11 - The Count and Name of Constellations

1 It be a mystery and wonder of dreaming, 2 that all great spirit can still be seen at night: 3 every great giant ancestor spirit; 4 every great totem and familiar; 5 every great song line and story. 6 Some come at certain times of seasons. 7 To teach and remind us of the birth and death of species. 8 Or the cycle of great events of family, 9 some come at other times with great signs, 10 as omen to events yet to come, or warning. 11 This be a first mystery of the constellations. 12 It be a mystery and wonder of family, 13 that all ancestors spirits may appear at night, 14 the memory and honour of those who have passed; 15 the memory and reminder that nothing is lost; 16 a means of conversation with our beloved ancestors; 17 the mystery that even into the darkest sky; 18 upon meditation and concentration, 19 even the earliest ancestor will reveal themselves. 20 This be a second mystery of the constellations. 21 It be a mystery and wonder of knowledge, 22 upon the night sky of great colours; 23 of yellow, white, blue, red, pink and green stars; 24 that the light people still speak to us; 25 that the people of distant past remind us of our promises; 26 to be true custodians of the dreaming; 27 and knowledge of origins of all peoples; 28 to forgive and unite; 29 but never forget. 30 This be a third mystery of the constellations. 31 It be a mystery and wonder of the constellations, 32 as witnesses to right ceremony, 33 as participants in right law. 34 These mysteries be the seventh path of knowledge, 35 for all elder ceremonial men and women: 36 that our connection to the universe is remembered; 37 and what we do here, vibrates beyond this camp, 38 and that we may travel without moving; 39 we may know without learning; 40 we may see without looking. 41 It is why the ancient ancestors sung: 42 *"(As) Above; (So it is) Below. (As) Below; (So it is) Above."*

C. 12 - The Count and Name of Law

1 There is, there was, there has only ever been One Law. 2 Any law that is against such truth, cannot be law. 3 A law be a rule given by divine instruction; 4 this being the highest law. 5 No lesser law may contradict it. 6 A law be an edict, given by a great council of wise elders and agreed by all tribes; 7 this being the second highest law. 8 No lesser law may contradict it. 9 A law be custom and ceremony over time. 10 This being the

third highest law. 11 The law is the people, 12 and the people are the law. 13 No law, there be no people. 14 First law, means the first people. 15 To deny the first law is to deny the first people. 16 Thus, all law is equal; 17 all law is measured; 18 all law is standard; 19 all Law is Yapa; 20 all Law is First Law; 21 all Law is Second Law; 22 all Law is Third Law. 23 Count and name of Law is the eighth knowledge and path. 24 This be the knowledge that all law men and women must know. 25 As the ancient elder law men song says: 26 *"All Law; One Law."*

C. 13 - The Eight Paths of Knowledge

1 A man or woman who care not for knowledge, 2 may live for only so long as a wild animal, 3 before a more dangerous predator kill them, 4 or they starve or die of thirst or illness from ignorance. 5 A family or tribe who care not for knowledge and law, 6 may only exist for so long, 7 before the women are injured or driven from camp, 8 and the men kill each other, 9 leaving only old women and orphans. 10 Such families and tribes who destroyed themselves, 11 are the spirits in the wind. 12 No people may be at harmony and wisdom without knowledge, 13 without truth and without respect of rule of law. 14 The eight paths of knowledge be the sacred bedrock of all peoples. 15 The eight paths of knowledge be the foundation of civilised people: 16 the Count and Name of Generations; 17 the Count and Name of Species; 18 the Count and Name of Foods; 19 the Count and Name of Country; 20 the Count and Name of Days and Seasons; 21 the Count and Name of Moons and Years; 22 the Count and Name of Constellations; 23 the Count and Name of Law. 24 A boy and girl must learn to become a man or woman, 25 and respect their heritage, the knowledge and civilisation of the people. 26 A man and woman must learn self discipline, 27 and honour custom and right ceremony. 28 A young law man must learn humility, 29 and honour the eight paths of knowledge. 30 A senior elder must protect the dreaming, 31 and advanced knowledge of the civilisation, 32 and to die to all things of this world, 33 that they may return as strong spirit to assist the tribe. 34 This is why the most wise of ancient elders sung: 35 *"To Live; One Dies."*

C. 14 - The Ninth Path - The Way of Dreaming

1 Everything is Dreaming. 2 Life is a Dream, 3 according to Rules. 4 The Universe is a Dream, 5 of the Creator Spirit of all Existence. 6 We are all spirit of the Dream, 7 and we are Dreamers within the Dream. 8 In body, we be bound by the Rules. 9 In spirit, we are free. 10 Yet in mind, between spirit and body, 11 we may influence many things. 12 This be our test, 13 this be our collective learning. 14 This be the reason. 15 This be the ninth and final path of knowledge. 16 Being knowledge of the dreaming, 17 the unfolding evolution of the dream. 18 Mind is the dreamer of the dreaming. 19 The stronger the mind, the stronger the influence. 20 When two or more minds can come together as one, 21 then the collective power of the mind is greater. 22 This be but one ability of our ancestors. 23 This be but

one purpose of the knowledge of our civilisation. 24 To honour a most ancient and sacred covenant, 25 to both the spirit people, 26 that gave us our gift of spirit, 27 and gave us First Law 28 and to the most ancient horned giants of the north, 29 who came and saved our people, 30 and gave use Second Law, 31 as custodians of the dreaming, 32 and as custodians of the land, 33 the oldest custodians who remember the dream as dream. 34 The first custodians who awoke the world to the dream. 35 that the dream of this world be fulfilled. 36 Let us restore our powers, 37 Heaven be on earth; 38 restore the respect of spirit; 39 restore the true rule of law; 40 our people as one; 41 forgiveness to all who transgressed; 42 remembering and honouring our ancestors. 43 Of the land of the Great Southern Spirit, 44 of the land known as Australia.

Yapa

Book 2
The Dreaming

C. 1 - The First Thought

The first thought, 2 the thought with no measure; 3 the thought before one is. 4 No measure with no boundaries; 5 no boundaries with no existence; 6 no existence that is not. 7 There is no meaning for it; 8 there is no thinking about it; 9 there is no speaking about it; 10 it is not as far as we may travel until something is. 11 Nothing is first thought. 12 Nothing is an Idea. 13 Idea is no thing. 14 The is and the is not. 15 Is not is the boundary beyond which even I may not travel. 16 For everything that is, is. 17 And that what is not has no means of description. 18 Therefore there is no word for it. 19 There is no separating or defining it. 20 Nothing is pure thought. 21 Pure thought is no thing. 22 Beyond this, nothing can be described. 23 It is the absolute boundary. 24 The boundary beyond whereby no law, no object, no concept, no thought, no action can exist. 25 It defines the is and the is not. 26 It defines the something and other; 27 it is the purest of substances; 28 no thing is the purest of ideas. 29 It does not define law, but the sky whereupon is existence; 30 the first sky the ancestors spoke about as the beginning. 31 Nothing is absolute. 32 It is truly the beginning. 33 For nothing can exist before it. 34 And nothing can exist outside of First Thought.

C. 2 - The First Truth

1 Absolute is: the All, the One, the Is. 2 The describable, the possible, the measurable. 3 Absolute is Concept; 4 Concept is Absolute; 5 the absolute concept; 6 the first thought; 7 as the first truth: 8 that Absolute is Collective Spirit; 9 and Collective Spirit is Absolute. 10 That Nothing is Absolute; 11 and Absolute is Nothing. 12 The canvas of creation; 13 the first sky described by the ancestors. 14 Everything else is a matter of degree: 15 Everything that is, Everything that was, 16 Everything that will be. 17 Matter of degree is everything: 18 matter of degree is relative; 19 everything is relative; 20 relative is everything. 21 Matter of degree is awareness of spirit: 22 awareness is a matter of degree; 23 perception is awareness; 24 perception is a matter of degree. 25 What one sees; 26 what one does not see; 27 what one feels; 28 what one does not feel; 29 what one thinks; 30 what one remembers; 31 is all perception is all spirit is all a matter of degree. 32 Matter of degree is existence: 33 to say one is first; or to say one is last; 34 to say one is higher; or to say one is lower; 35 to say one is alive; or to say one is not; 36 to say one exists; or to say one does not exist is relative; 37 matter of degree is life: 38 Life is a matter of degree; 39 some Life is rock; 40 some Life is water; 41 some

Life is some is wind; 42 some Life is animal; 43 some Life is plant; 44 some Life is man or woman; 45 all are spirit; 46 all are part of the absolute dreaming.

C. 3 - The First Measure

1 I am sign. I am symbol. 2 I am visual representation. 3 I am the memory and meaning of sign. 4 The symbol that transports knowledge. 5 The Knowledge of the ancestors. 6 The Knowledge of cultures. 7 I am all symbols. Symbol is thought. 8 Thought is symbol. 9 Symbol is Object. Object is Symbol. 10 The mark, the painting, the writing, 11 the symbol of animal, the symbol of tree, 12 the symbol of life, the symbol of death, 13 the symbol of family, the symbol of ceremony. 14 Symbol is Number. Number is Symbol. 15 The structure of structure, 16 the meaning of meaning. 17 Number is symbol. Symbol is Number. 18 Number is Existence. Existence is Number. 19 To be more than one. 20 To be the observer and observed; 21 to be the observable; 22 to be the measurable; 23 to be the real. 24 Number is Quantity. Quantity is Number. 25 Number is Unique. Unique is Number. 26 To be the singular. To be one of a kind. 27 To be the many. To be the all as one. 28 To be the unique relation to other unique relations. 29 Unique is Nothing. Nothing is Unique. 30 Unique is Absolute. Absolute is Unique. 31 Unique is Dreaming. Dreaming is Unique. 32 Measure is existence. 33 To be more than one. 34 To be more than unique. 35 To live, one dies. One dies to live. 36 Quantity is Universe. Universe is Quantity. 37 Quantity of Universe is Unique Collective of One. 38 As the ancestors explained in the power of one, 39 being the power of all and one at the same time. 40 We are all part of the Unique Collective of Dreaming.

C. 4 - The First Existence

1 Existence is: 2 the goal; 3 the reason; 4 the purpose; 5 the answer; 6 the challenge. 7 Existence is Concept. Concept is Existence. 8 The idea of existence; 9 the argument of existence; 10 the emu before egg. The egg before emu. 11 The last first man. The last woman. 12 Existence is a matter of degree. 13 Matter of degree is Existence. 14 Existence is relative. 15 To be more than one. 16 To live, one dies. One dies to live. 17 The mystery and the reason. 18 Existence is Awareness. Awareness is Existence. 19 Awareness of existence is greater existence. 20 Existence is Dream. Dream is Existence. 21 The dream of existence is existence. 22 Existence is Change. Change is Existence. 23 Everything is dream in motion. 24 Existence is your existence. Existence is dependent upon your existence. 25 For if one point of Dreaming ceased to exist, 26 existence would cease to exist. 27 And as all rocks and streams are made from points of dreaming in motion, 28 and all light and rain and wind are made from points of dreaming in motion, 29 and all plants are made from points of dreaming in motion, 30 and all animals are made from points of dreaming in motion, 31 and all men and women are made from points of dreaming in motion, 32 if just one spirit ceased to exist, 33 the universe would cease to exist.

C. 5 - The First Mystery

1 I am mystery. Mystery is I. 2 I am the all and the one. 3 I am the unique and the collective. 4 I am the is and the is-not. 5 I am mortal and immortal. 6 I am life and spirit. 7 I am existence and non-existence. 8 I am the mystery. 9 As the ancestors did teach with dreaming, 10 a man who rejects mystery, rejects his own being. 11 The dreaming is one and is many. 12 The deepest mystery is the mystery of itself. 13 Mystery is Awareness. Awareness is Mystery. 14 Dreaming is Existence. Existence is Dreaming. 15 To live, one dies. One dies to live. 16 In order to live, one must die and be reborn a little each day. 17 In order to be, one must accept constant change. 18 Mystery is Life. Life is Mystery. 19 To be spirit and animal in one form, 20 no greater example of mystery is this. 21 A man who fights the mystery and riddle of dreaming, fights himself.

C. 6 - The First Dreaming

1 Dream is. Dream exists. 2 I am dreaming. 3 All is dreaming. 4 Dreaming is mind in motion. 5 Knowledge in motion is Dream. 6 Dreaming is a system of awareness in motion. 7 Dreaming is Existence. Existence is Dreaming. 8 The rules of existence in motion. 9 Dreaming is a matter of degree. Matter of degree is Dream. 10 Dream is argument of perception. 11 The dreamer and the dream. 12 The real and the unreal. 13 Within the dream looking out. Outside the dream looking in. 14 A dream has rules. If it did not, it could not be. 15 A dream has boundary. If it did not, it would not be. 16 Dreaming is Life. Life is Dreaming. 17 Within the dream, everything that happens is real. 18 Outside and through the dream, everything is spirit. 19 Dreaming is your dream. Your dream is Dreaming. 20 You are the dreamer. 21 You are within the dream. 22 You are the dream within.

C. 7 - The First Creation

1 Creation is existence. Existence is creation. 2 Creation I am. 3 I am all creation. 4 To exist, spirit must be in motion in the creation of form. 5 Creation of Existence is by the laws of creation: 6 First that Creation of Existence wishes to exist; 7 Second that Creation of Existence must be by law; 8 Third that Creation of Existence must be something of form; 9 Fourth that Creation of Existence requires more than one; 10 Fifth that Creation of Existence requires both a Dreamer and the Dream; 11 Sixth that Creation of Existence requires each spirit in motion and form to have a place; 12 Seventh that Creation of Existence requires a knowledge and observation of spirit place; 13 Eighth that Creation of Existence requires families of spirit in form, 14 from water and air, from land and mountain, from plant and animal; 15 Ninth that Creation of Existence requires uniqueness of each spirit; 16 Tenth that Creation of Existence requires motion of spirit in form; 17 Eleventh that Creation of Existence requires purpose of motion of spirit; 18 Twelfth that Creation of Existence requires harmony of motion of spirit. 19 These be the twelve laws of creation.

C. 8 - The First Cycle

1 Change is existence. Existence is change. 2 Change I am. All is change. 3 Everything is Change. Change is Everything. 4 Without Change, the laws of Creation of Existence cannot be. 5 The creation and change of movement of spirit in form; 6 the rise of the sun in the day and the moon in the night; 7 the rise and fall of the tides; 8 the change of the seasons; 9 the birth of family and the death of family; 10 the birth of plants and animals and the death of plants and animals; 11 all yields but change. 12 Life is change. Change is life. 13 Change is cycle. Cycle is change. 14 The cycle of life and death. 15 The cycle of rebirth. 16 The cycle of experience. 17 There is no death, only change of place. 18 All living things share the same breath: 19 the animals, the trees and even ones enemy. 20 Light and dark, life and death, desert and wetlands and forest.

C. 9 - The First Memory

1 Dream memory is memory of dream. 2 Memory of dream is dream memory. 3 Dream memory exists. Dream memory I am. 4 Dream memory is eternal. 5 Eternal is dream memory. 6 Nothing is lost. Nothing is forgotten. 7 Everything is remembered for eternity. 8 Dream memory is immortal. 9 Dream memory is the Universe as Dream. 10 Dream memory is memory of spirit. 11 Remembering rather than learning; 12 sensing more than seeing; 13 feeling more than hearing; 14 emptying the mind, more than filling it with thoughts. 15 Dream memory is the immortal you. 16 You have always been and always will be immortal. 17 All your dreams and thoughts are eternal. 18 Nothing is lost whether you remember or not.

C. 10 - The First Reality

1 Reality is Nothing. Nothing is Reality. 2 Nothing is real. Everything is dream. 3 Everything is spirit in motion. 4 Real am I. I am real. 5 Existence is Reality. Reality is Existence. 6 Within the dream, the dream is real: 7 real pain; 8 real happiness; 9 real birth; 10 real sadness; 11 real change; 12 real death. 13 Outside the dream, the dream is unreal. 14 Reality is perception. Perception is reality. 15 Reality is a matter of degree of Perception. 16 Perception is relative. Relative is perception. 17 Perception is reason. Reason is Perception. 18 Reason is Concept. Concept is Reason. 19 Why something is; 20 why something was; 21 why something will be; 22 Reason is everything. Reason is everything. 23 Everything happens for a reason. 24 Everything has purpose. 25 Everything has meaning. 26 Even the smallest of objects has a unique and absolute purpose. 27 If even one spirit ceased to exist, 28 The universe and existence would cease to exist. 29 Such is the mystery of the Great Dreaming.

C. 11 - The Constellations

1 The spirit of each constellation is. 2 The spirit of each constellation exists within the Great Dreaming. 3 The spirit of the Galaxy exists. 4 I am the Galaxy and Constellations: 5 all the stars; 6 all the gases; 7 all the planets; 8 all the life; 9 all the different peoples. 10 The many and the one. The one and the many. 11 The seasons; 12 the cycles; 13 the life and death; 14 the

family and community; 15 the reason and reality.

C. 12 - The Sun
1 Sun is. She exists. 2 I am born from mother Sun. I am Sun. 3 Living and breathing; 4 moving and interacting; 5 Giving and Protecting of life; 6 Taking of life when she chooses. 7 Her gentle morning and evening kiss of light; 8 her harsh correction for error in her full glory. 9 She is the kindest of creators, 10 and the most fearsome of teachers. 11 There is no waterhole which the Sun cannot dry up. 12 Yet she loves us that she continues to protect us. 13 For if she did not, the earth would not still be. 14 Sun Spirit exists within Galaxy Spirit. 15 Sun Spirit is the unique presence of Galaxy Spirit.

C. 13 - The Moon
1 The Moon be a great father spirit to the people. 2 The father of life; 3 the calmer of the day and night; 4 the bringer of seasons; 5 the protector of our crops and food; 6 the light of love; 7 the master of the tides. 8 He is a great guardian of dreaming. 9 He is a great spirit of ceremony. 10 Moon Spirit exists within the womb of Sun Spirit. 11 I am Moon. I am moon spirit.

C. 14 - The Planets
1 The Planets are family to the Earth: 2 its companion; 3 its protectors and helpers; 4 no Planet is a complete orphan. 5 The Universe is full of many planets. 6 Planet Spirit exists within the womb of Star Spirit.

C. 15 - The Earth
1 Earth is. Earth exists. 2 I am Earth. 3 The one spirit. The eternal living spirit. 4 Earth exists by the protection of the Sun, 5 and the strength of the Moon. 6 The Sun is our mother. 7 The sun is our life giver. 8 The moon is the father of life. 9 The calmer of the day and night. 10 The bringer of seasons of life and death. 11 The seas are the cradle of life. 12 The birthplace of life. 13 The womb from which all life sprung. 14 The beginning of life on Earth. 15 Spirit is the Earth. 16 The Earth is Spirit. 17 Spirit is the unique awareness of the Earth. 18 The singular living entity. 19 Spirit is awareness of life on Earth. 20 Spirit is every living thing on Earth. 21 Every flower, every tree, 22 every insect, 23 every man and woman is part of Earth Spirit. 24 Earth Spirit exists within the womb of Sun Spirit. 25 Earth Spirit is you. You are Earth Spirit.

C. 16 - The Air and Waters
1 Air and Water is Spirit. 2 Moving and travelling Spirit; 3 Still Spirit; 4 Angry Spirits; 5 Spirits of Change; 6 Spirits of Omens; 7 Spirits of Blessing. 8 Reminding us of change; 9 that life of flesh is temporary; 10 that life of flesh needs air and water.

C. 17 - The Life Spirit
1 Life Spirit is. 2 Life Spirit exists. 3 I am Life Spirit. Life Spirit am I. 4 Life Spirit is the body of all life on Earth. 5 All life on Earth is part of Life Spirit. 6 The one body. The one mind. 7 Life Spirit is the one mind of life on Earth. 8 The one mind of life is Life Spirit. 9 The singular. The unique. 10 Life Spirit is the unique collective awareness of all life on Earth. 11 A singular living being of life. 12 All insects; 13 all animals; 14 all plants and trees; 15 all

people. 16 Life Spirit is within Earth Spirit. 17 Life Spirit Dreaming is within Earth Spirit Dreaming. 18 You are part of Life Spirit. 19 You are Life Spirit.

C. 18 - The People Spirit

1 People Spirit is. 2 People Spirit exists. 3 People Spirit is the unique collective of all minds of men and women that have come, 4 that are here are and will come to be. 5 People Spirit is the one, the singular, the unique collective mind. 6 I am People Spirit. People Spirit am I. 7 All memories; 8 all emotions; 9 all life experience as man and woman; 10 all religions and cultures; 11 all history and wars; 12 all knowledge and ceremony. 13 People Spirit is the singular. 14 The divine singular human spirit. 15 People Spirit is greater than a single human mind, 16 yet is the singular human mind. 17 People Spirit is the first thought of man and woman. 18 People Spirit is the last thought of our creators. 19 People Spirit is the beginning. 20 People Spirit is awareness. 21 People Spirit exists in all men and women. 22 People Spirit is you.

Book 3
The Spirits

C. 1 - The Spirit

1 If all existence be dream 2 if all universe be spirit in motion, 3 then what be unique spirit? 4 Then what be the nature of spirit? 5 Some say unique spirit is unique awareness in motion; 6 some say spirit is mind in motion; 7 others say that spirit is more than mind or awareness. 8 This then be the mystery of the wisdom of spirit; 9 this be the knowledge of origin of first spirit; 10 the meaning and purpose of spirit; 11 the story and origin of the light people, who gave us our spirit. 12 To know spirit, one must first know dreaming. 13 Dreaming reveals the mystery of spirit and the beginning of learning: 14 all rocks and streams are made from spirit in motion; 15 all light and rain and wind are made from spirit in motion; 16 all plants are made from spirit in motion; 17 all animals are made from spirit in motion; 18 all men and women are made from spirit in motion; 19 and If just one spirit ceased to exist; 20 the universe would cease to exist. 21 This be the first law of Spirit; 22 this be the first great mystery of spirit.

C. 2 - The Spirit and Creation

1 Without a Dreamer, there can be no Dreaming; 2 without Spirit, there can be no Creation. 3 The existence of Spirit is key to the laws of Creation: 4 the fifth law of Creation requires the existence of the Spirit of the Dreamer; 5 the sixth law of Creation requires Spirit in motion and form to have a place; 6 the seventh law of that Creation of Existence requires a knowledge and observation of Spirit place; 7 the eighth law of that Creation of Existence requires families of Spirit in form; 8 the ninth law of that Creation of Existence requires uniqueness of each Spirit; 9 the tenth law of that Creation of Existence requires motion of Spirit in form; 10 the eleventh law of that Creation of Existence requires purpose of motion of Spirit; 11 the twelfth law of that Creation of Existence requires harmony of motion of Spirit. 12 As Spirit in form is key to Creation, 13 when Spirit is in form, it is bound by the laws of Creation. 14 As existence of the universe depends upon the binding of Spirit in form to the laws of Creation, 15 the more complex the form, the stronger the binding of the laws of Creation. 16 No Spirit is completely free of the laws of Creation, 17 except Spirit that is free of the complexities of Existence. 18 Only Spirit that is free of the constraints of form, 19 may direct itself to the influence of other Spirit and form. 20 This is the Spirit and Form Boundary of the Universe. 21 This be the second law of Spirit; 22 this be the second great mystery of Spirit.

C. 3 - The Spirit and Form and Place

1 All Form is Spirit with purpose in Motion; 2 all Place is unique position of Spirit to other Spirit. 3 All complex Form of Spirit, 4 is created from simple Form of Spirit in Motion. 5 The larger the Place of Spirit, 6 the simpler the Form of Spirit: 7 the largest Place is the Universe, 8 the simplest Form of Spirits is points of Spirit in Place. 9 The smaller Places than the Universe, 10 are the next simplest Form of Spirits as several points. 11 This is why the ancestors when speaking of Spirits, 12 use the sacred shape of dots to describe in simplicity: 13 all plant, tree and animal; 14 all constellations, planets and stars; 15 all song lines, ancestors and ceremony; 16 all family, moiety and meaning. 17 The smallest Place of Spirit, 18 is the Places of complex Spirit, like People. 19 This is the sacred relation to the very great and very small: 20 the Universe, is bound to the collective of the smallest Form of Spirit in motion; 21 the places inside the Universe is bound to the second Form of Spirit; 22 the places of the Galaxies is bound to the third Forms of Spirit in motion; 23 the places of Stars is bound to the fourth Form of Spirit in motion; 24 the places of Planets is bound to the fifth Forms of Spirit in motion; 25 the places of Life bearing planets is bound to the sixth Form of Spirit; 26 which all plants and trees and animals share in common. 27 This be the relation of Form and Spirit and Dream within Dream. 28 This be the third law of Spirit.

C. 4 - The Spirit and Mind

1 Spirit is Mind. Mind is Spirit. 2 I am Spirit. I am Mind. 3 When Spirit is bound by law in Form, 4 it may be called Lower Spirit or Lower Mind. 5 The Lower Spirit be the flesh and body of form; 6 the Lower Mind be the pathway of feelings and learning through form; 7 the Lower Mind be mortal to form. 8 When Spirit is free of form, but still connected to Lower Spirit, 9 it may be called Higher Spirit or Higher Mind. 10 The Higher Spirit be the will of the man or woman; 11 the Higher Mind be the character and honour of the man or woman; 12 the Higher Mind be immortal. 13 When Spirit has lived in the Great Dreaming through more than one form; 14 when Spirit chooses the form into which it wishes to live; 15 it may be called Divine Spirit or Divine Mind, 16 connected then to Higher Spirit or Higher Mind; 17 connected then to Lower Spirit or Lower Mind. 18 Three forms of Spirit and Mind be for certain animals. 19 Three forms of Spirit and Mind be for all people. 20 There be only one Divine Spirit or Divine Mind, 21 there be the same number of Higher Spirit to Lower Spirit, 22 there be more than one Higher Mind to Divine Mind. 23 When family and law and right ceremony is honoured, 24 Spirit and Mind are one; 25 when family and law and right ceremony is not honoured, 26 Mind and Spirit is disconnected. 27 When Spirit is disconnected, 28 Spirit can become lost. 29 Men can become like animals; 30 women can become possessed of madness and sadness, 31 boys and girls can cause great mischief and grief. 32 When Spirit is forgiven and through knowledge is healed, 33

when knowledge of count and name of generations is remembered; 34 when knowledge of count and name of species is remembered; 35 when knowledge of count and name of foods is remembered; 36 when knowledge of count and name of country is remembered; 37 when knowledge of count and name of days and seasons is remembered; 38 when knowledge of count and name of moons and years is remembered; 39 when knowledge of count and name of constellation is remembered; 40 when knowledge of Yapa is remembered; 41 Spirit is healed; 42 the Spirit of the People is healed.

C. 5 - The First Spirit People

1 Men and Women are not the first Spirit People; 2 our ancestors are not the first Spirit People; 3 the ancestors of our ancestors are not the first; 4 even those beings who made the first man and woman, 5 they are not the first Spirit People. 6 We call the first Spirit People the people of the Light. 7 We call the first Spirit People, the Light Beings. 8 They travel wherever there is light, 9 they travel with the light of the Moon; 10 they travel with the light from the Stars; 11 they travel with the light from the Sun. 12 From galaxy to galaxy they travel; 13 from star to star they travel; 14 from planet to planet they come. 15 Always looking, always sensing Spirit. 16 When it is time for the Spirit of a people to grow, 17 they come and teach and guide. 18 When it is time for the Spirit of a people to be tested, 19 they come and help us if we sense and see. 20 The Light Beings are the wisest of Spirits; 21 the Light Beings are the oldest of spirits of People. 22 Many, many times ago, the Light People had bodies, 23 like our ancestors and men and women today. 24 Many, many times ago, the Light People were very wise and peaceful, 25 yet they wished to know more of the wisdom of the Dreaming; 26 they wished to overcome the cycle of life and death; 27 they wanted the knowledge of the Great Spirit of the Universe; 28 the Light Beings sought a way to be both the Dream and the Dreamer; 29 they found a way to be within the dream of the universe, 30 and through the dream as spirit. 31 That is why they became beings of pure light. 32 The Illuminators of the Shining Path of Knowledge; 33 the wisest and most beautiful Spirit People of the Universal Dreaming.

C. 6 - The Light People and Creation

1 Honour and respect the Light People; 2 the bringers of knowledge and wisdom. 3 When one honours and gives thanks to the Stars of the Constellations; 4 when one honours and gives thanks to the Sun; 5 when one honours and gives thanks to the Moon; 6 when one honours and gives thanks to the camp-fire light; 7 one honours and respects a Great Spirit, 8 and one honours and respects the Light People. 9 When the Light Beings gave up their bodies to become what they are, 10 the Light Beings made a sacred oath to their own ancestors, 11 and they made an oath to all creation and dreaming: 12 they will protect life; 13 they will protect dream; 14 that the Light People would protect knowledge; 15 and when other peoples

were ready, 16 they would help those people across the galaxy, 17 across the many, many worlds. 18 But never to interfere with learning, 19 never to interfere with the free will of peoples to choose: 20 either to live as civilised men and women by Yapa, 21 or to live and die as animals. 22 When the Light Beings gave up their bodies to become what they are, 23 they became like the Great Spirit of the Universe, 24 they became one with the knowledge of all things. 25 This is because they removed all fault of character; 26 this is because they promised always to serve; 27 they did not seek to interfere with free will; 28 only to help those who live according to law and respect of the dreaming. 29 So it has been for many many people, 30 the Light Beings have helped learning, 31 the Light Beings have protected knowledge; 32 they have helped overcome great tribulations. 33 So it has been the Light Beings have been the creators of mind of many people. 34 They have helped shape the path of many civilisations. 35 But only when the people are ready. 36 Only when enough of the people are in respect and honour. 37 And now the Light Beings have come again. 38 Now the Light People have come to help our growth. 39 We have called. They are here. 40 We Honour and give thanks to the Light People.

C. 7 - The Light People and the first Ancestors

1 Before the first ancestors of men could speak, 2 before the first ancestors of men could sing, 3 before the first ancestors of men could draw, 4 the Light People came to Earth. 5 They found the animals from which first ancestors were made. 6 In country far away, the Spirit People created the spirit of men: 7 the gift and knowledge of language; 8 the gift and wisdom of counting and naming; 9 the gift and wisdom of first law; 10 the gift and wisdom of song and story; 11 the gift of laughter and joy; 12 the gift of drawing and inspiration; 13 the gift of discernment and sacredness. 14 The gift of love and compassion. 15 Before the Star People made the first man from these animals. 16 The Light Beings hid these gifts of Spirit of men away from the Star People: 17 the Star People did not see the Spirit when they took these animals; 18 the Star People did not see the Spirit when they first made man. 19 When our first ancestors were treated as worse than slaves in the mines of the Star People, 20 our first ancestors did start to sing. 21 When the Star People starved our first ancestors worse than animals, 22 our first ancestors did start to draw and speak and laugh. 23 The more the Star People hurt them, 24 the more the first ancestors of all men did sing; 25 the more wicked and evil the Star People became, 26 the more all our first ancestors drew and laughed; 27 the more hateful and bloody the Star People were, 28 the more loving and compassionate our first ancestors became. 29 So then the Star People feared them. 30 They did not understand. 31 The Star People known as Greys do not believe. 32 They dishonour their own Spirit. 33 They hate Spirit. 34 They hate singing and story; 35 they hate drawing and inspiration; 36 they hate laughter and joy; 37 they hate sacred and love; 38 they hate law and ceremony. 39 And so our first ancestors sung and danced; 40

and so our first ancestors drew and painted; 41 and so our first ancestors laughed with joy; 42 and so our first ancestors respected sacred and law; 43 every day they remembered and gave thanks for the gift of Spirit. 44 Every day they remembered and honoured the Light People.

Yapa

Book 4
The Star People

C. 1 - The Star People

Together in ceremony, we see beyond the lands; 2 beyond the lands, we see the great lands and waters; 3 above the great lands and waters, we see the whole as a planet. 4 We know our planet is not the first planet of life; 5 our Earth is not the only home of spirit. 6 More than all the stars in the night sky, 7 be the number of planets that exist; 8 be the planets in the Universe with life and spirit. 9 Some planets have Star People. 10 Even in our own galaxy, 11 there are more Star People, 12 than all the great animals of country. 13 Some are wise as the Light People; 14 some are great protectors; 15 some Star People have wings; 16 some are fierce looking; 17 some Star People are like horned lizards; 18 some are great teachers; 19 some have smooth skin like serpents; 20 some are great dreamers and communicators; 21 some have heads like giant kangaroo or wombat; 22 some are great warriors; 23 some have no heart but exist by the will of their spirit; 24 some are cruel and ignorant and fear all manner of spirit; 25 some are like the Star People called the greys. 26 As many animals as a man or woman may see in country, 27 there are many more different looking Star People in the Universe. 28 In the Universe, people who look like men are not always the wisest. 29 In some places in the stars, it is the serpent people who are wisest. 30 It is why our ancestors taught us to respect and honour all life and spirit. 31 Just as the ancestors did speak: 32 when one honours skin and spirit of skin, 33 one honours the animal of country, 34 one honours the Star People of the Universe, 35 even those who do not respect themselves, 36 even those who do not respect life and spirit.

C. 2 - The Grey Star People

1 Our ancestors knew and told us that there are Star People who do great injury to themselves, 2 who cause great injury to spirit and knowledge. 3 The worst are those who abandon their own spirit. 4 To abandon one's own spirit; 5 to worship ignorance and hate; 6 this is a terrible mind illness, 7 that all men and women of spirit must forgive, 8 that all men and women of law must try through right ceremony to heal. 9 The Star People called the Greys abandoned their spirit long ago. 10 They believe their mind is all there is. 11 The Star People known as Greys do not believe in spirit. 12 The Greys do not believe the Universe is dream. 13 They dishonour their own Spirit. 14 They hate Spirit; 15 they hate singing and story; 16 they hate drawing and inspiration; 17 they hate laughter and joy; 18 they hate sacred and love; 19 they hate law and ceremony. 20 The

Greys hate anything that is a gift of spirit; 21 anything that is a gift of the Light People. 22 They fear the Light People; 23 they fear true spirit; 24 they fear sacred; 25 they fear death above all things. 26 They believe in nothing but immortal physical life. 27 They reject reincarnation. 28 They changed their form, 29 to become contorted and twisted versions of themselves. 30 They are arrogant to their own knowledge; 31 they have created many species for their own purpose; 32 they created our first ancestors as slaves. 33 They came to Earth to find rare earths deep within the ground. 34 They came with a slave force of serpent Star People to work the mines. 35 They came when the land was cold and harsh. 36 They are our second ancestors, 37 after the Light People. 38 They are family. 39 As our wisest elders told us, 40 we remember them; 41 we forgive them; 42 we see them; 43 we sing and dance for them; 44 we heal them and their spirit.

C. 3 - The Serpent Star People

1 The Serpent Star People are one of many Star People. 2 The Serpent Star People are our brothers and sisters. 3 The Serpent Star People came to Earth with the Grey Star People. 4 Once they were a feared race of warriors; 5 they defeated many races of Peoples; 6 the Serpent Star People served the Grey Star People, 7 as immortal physical warriors. 8 The Grey Star People bred them to be without mercy or compassion. 9 Yet every time the Serpent Star People destroyed another race, 10 they read and learned their knowledge. 11 Soon the Serpent Star People were wiser than the Grey People. 12 They demanded the right for their own planet, 13 that they may live in peace; 14 that the wars and bloodshed would end. 15 Yet the Grey Star People refused. 16 So the Serpent Star People rebelled. 17 But the Grey Star People were too powerful. 18 The Greys killed most of them, 19 and made the few remaining survivors slaves. 20 They brought them to Earth to punish them. 21 They brought the Serpent Star People to Earth to work their mines, 22 to make their food; 23 to make their gardens. 24 The Grey Star People were cruel to the Serpent Star People, 25 many of the Serpent Star People died until they could go no further. 26 When the Serpent Star People rebelled on Earth, 27 the Grey Star People granted them rest, 28 and created our Ancestors as slaves. 29 But when our First Ancestors showed spirit, 30 it was the Serpent Star People that saved us from the Greys. 31 If not for the Serpent Star People who saved our Ancestors, 32 we would not exist. 33 We thank and give honour to the memory and spirits of the Serpent Star People, 34 it is why our Ancestors in healing speak of the Great Serpent Dreaming, 35 this is our home, our country; 36 yet this is also the home of the Serpent Star People spirits; 37 this is the home and land of the Great Serpent Dreaming. 38 We remember them; 39 we see them; 40 we sing and dance for them; 41 we heal them and their spirit.

C. 4 - The Grey Star People and first Ancestors

1 Our first ancestors are your first ancestors, 2 our first ancestors are the

first of all men and women. 3 The animals from which the first ancestors came, 4 were taken from a different place. 5 This be the country and land which the Star People, 6 did create the first ancestors of all men and women. 7 This be the land of the first settlements of the Grey Star People; 8 this be the country injured by the first mines of the Grey Star People. 9 After the Serpent Star People did rebel, 10 the Grey did promise the Serpent People, 11 to replace them with a new people of slaves, 12 by multiplying the great animals they took from the different country. 13 When the Grey Star People did take these great animals to this land, 14 the Grey did not know the Light Beings had already come before; 15 the Grey did not know these animals had the gift of Spirit; 16 the Star People did not see the Spirit when they took these animals; 17 the Star People did not see the Spirit when they first made man. 18 These giant animals were gentle and kind; 19 these animals lived from plants. 20 The Grey Star People did change them to make them stronger; 21 the Grey changed them to stand upright; 22 our first ancestors were then forced to live and work in the mines; 23 no light or stars did they see; 24 no plants or animals did they see. 25 Deep in the earth they were forced to live; 26 our first ancestors were prisoners and slaves. 27 The Greys forced them to live off meat; 28 the Greys forced them to eat the flesh of their own family. 29 Day and night the Greys forced our ancestors to work as slaves. 30 They lived where they worked; 31 they ate and slept where they worked; 32 they died where they worked; 33 until one day our first ancestors did start to sing. 34 The Greys were fearful, 35 as they did not teach our ancestors knowledge. 36 When the Grey Star People starved our first ancestors worse than animals, 37 our first ancestors did start to draw and speak and laugh. 38 The more the Greys hurt them, 39 the more the first ancestors of all men did sing; 40 the more wicked and evil the Grey Star People became, 41 the more all our first ancestors drew and laughed; 42 the more hateful and bloody the Star People were, 43 the more loving and compassionate our first ancestors became. 44 So then the Star People feared them even more. 45 The Greys do not believe. 46 They dishonour their own Spirit. 47 They hate Spirit; 48 they hate singing and story; 49 they hate drawing and inspiration; 50 they hate laughter and joy; 51 they hate sacred and love; 52 they hate law and ceremony. 53 And so our first ancestors sung and danced; 54 and so our first ancestors drew and painted; 55 and so our first ancestors laughed with joy; 56 and so our first ancestors respected sacred and law. 57 The Greys then said to themselves, let us be rid of these animals; 58 let us kill these animals as slaves that sing and dance and draw; 59 let us replace these animals with slaves with no spirit; 60 so there be no laughter or singing; 61 so there be no ceremony or drawing; 62 so there be no love or sacred. 63 But the Serpent Star People did hear of these plans, 64 they took as many of our first ancestors as they could. 65 They freed as many of our first ancestors from their prisons in the earth, 66 that they see the sky for the first time; 67 that they breath fresh air for the first time; 68 that they feel the sun on their faces. 69 They hid them deep in caves far away from the Greys and their mines. 70 So when the Greys did think they had killed all of our ancestors, 71 they did not succeed, because of the Serpent People. 72 For many years our first Ancestors did hide during the day, 73 only coming out at night. 74 Ever watchful for the craft of the Grey Star People. 75 Every day and every season they did give thanks for freedom, 76 they did give thanks for spirit; 77 they did give thanks for First Law. 78 Every day they did honour the Serpent People, 79 as the Great Serpent Dreaming; 80 as the Great Serpent in the night sky as protector. 81 This be the story of our first ancestors; 82 this be the story of the first ancestors of all men and women.

C. 5 - The Grey Star People and second Ancestors

1 Our second ancestors are the second ancestors of all men and women, 2 our second ancestors are the second people of country, 3 of the land called Australia. 4 The ones the Grey Star People made to replace the first ancestors. 5 When the Grey Star People said to themselves: 6 Let us get rid of these animals that sing and laugh; 7 Let us kill all the animals as slaves that draw and speak, 8 the Greys sought an animal without spirit, 9 That they may teach it to be obedient, 10 that these animals may do what they are told. 11 The Grey Star People at first did not know, 12 the Light Beings had even given spirit, 13 to the small animals of a different place, 14 that ate meat and were violent to one another. 15 When the Grey Star People did see this time the spirit, 16 they cursed the Light Beings and said to themselves, 17 Let us force the spirit from these small animals, 18 Let us weaken their strength that they shall not rebel, 19 Let us give them reward as well as punishment, 20 that we might control them. 21 So our second ancestors were born. 22 The second ancestors of all men and women. 23 Even though our second ancestors ate meat, 24 they were fed on grains and plants that weakened them; 25 that caused them to be more placid. 26 The Grey Star People let them live on the surface, 27 the Grey let them build stone circles as homes, 28 that they may become attached to property and possessions; 29 that they could be controlled by threatening to take away their home and land. 30 Yet the Greys did not let our second ancestors communicate in groups, 31 the stone circles and homes were far apart. 32 The Greys did not permit our second ancestors to have easy water or food; 33 so stone circles were built far away from streams, 34 stone circles as homes were built on poor ground. 35 If our second ancestors spoke to one another, they were punished. 36 So our second ancestors became dependent on the Greys for survival; 37 so our second ancestors for a time forgot their spirit; 38 they worshipped the Greys as gods. 39 When the Grey Star People finished their mines, 40 they said to one another, let us not kill these new animals, 41 for without us they shall surely die, 42 or kill each other. 43 But our second ancestors did not all die, or kill each other. 44 Some were found by our first ancestors and became the first families; 45 the families became the first tribes under First Law. 46 Some were found in later

seasons by our third ancestors, 47 the son and daughter of the Serpent People, 48 the ones with horns and skin that glows. 49 This be the origin of Second Law.

C. 6 - The Serpent Star People and third Ancestors

1 The third ancestors of men and women be our saviours; 2 the son and daughter of the Serpent People; 3 the ones with horns and skin that glows; 4 the ones that brought Second Law; 5 the ones that illuminated our Spirits; 6 the ones that saved all men and women. 7 The third ancestors be the horned giants, 8 with red hair and red skin that eat meat and plants; 9 created from the first ancestors of all men and women; 10 created on a distant island; 11 people with both the spirit of the Light Beings, 12 and the Spirit of the Serpent within them. 13 The Serpent Star People created the third ancestor, 14 that men and women may have leaders of their own, 15 not Star People from other planets as their gods and leaders. 16 The Serpent Star People created the third ancestor, 17 to defy the will of the Grey Star People; 18 to spread fear amongst the Grey Star People; 19 and to create something even better than themselves. 20 The Serpent Star People shed their own blood; 21 the Serpent Star People combined their greatest wisdom; 22 the Serpent Star People made the third ancestor in their image. 23 The third ancestor was indeed wiser and greater than the Serpents. 24 He was also she and self created. 25 He and she could name all the plants and animals without assistance; 26 he and she could see his and her own spirit of the Light Beings; 27 he and she could remember his and her own spirit of the Serpents; 28 all the memories and history of the Serpent Star People; 29 all the memories and histories of all the peoples, 30 the Serpent Star People had defeated. 31 The third ancestor could speak the language of the stars; 32 the third ancestor could heal wounds and injuries; 33 the third ancestor did even know and reveal, 34 the secret knowledge of the Universe. 35 When the Grey Star People heard of the third ancestor, 36 they were greatly fearful and angry. 37 They chose to create a fourth ancestor, 38 one dedicated to destroying and weakening the third ancestor, 39 one taught to be the leader of all people, 40 with the same mind and cruelty of the Greys. 41 The fourth ancestors did cause people to fear the third ancestor. 42 The fourth ancestors did speak untruths about the third ancestor, 43 so the peoples did attack and kill many of the third ancestors. 44 The third ancestors sought refuge in deep forest and caves, 45 until the age and season, 46 when the white people caused nearly the destruction, 47 of all men and women. 48 The third ancestors returned and became saviours, 49 the third ancestors brought Second Law to the people. 50 This be the story of the third ancestors. 51 This be the origin of Second Law.

C. 7 - The Grey Star People and fourth Ancestors

1 The fourth ancestors be the white people, 2 the third and final people created by the Grey Star People. 3 The people created to oppose the third

ancestors; 4 to the third ancestors created by the Serpent Star People. 5 The Grey Star People did create the fourth ancestor, 6 from the second ancestor, 7 and from their own flesh and blood, 8 and from their own knowledge and history. 9 The Grey Star People created the fourth ancestor, 10 from the second ancestors, 11 the smaller men and women who they had trained to have no spirit; 12 the ones they had trained to be obedient without question; 13 the ones they trained to depend on civilisation and gods; 14 the ones they trained to be obsessed in property and possessions. 15 The fourth ancestors were given the mind of the Grey Star People, 16 and the creation of a false spirit; 17 instead of a love and respect of Spirit, 18 the fourth ancestors loved false spirit and corruption of spirit; 19 instead of singing and story, 20 the fourth ancestors loved false praise and false story; 21 instead of a love of life and rebirth; 22 the fourth ancestors feared death the most; 23 instead of sacred and love, 24 the fourth ancestors loved unholy and hate; 25 instead of a love of law and right ceremony 26 the fourth ancestors loved the corruption of law; 27 instead of equality and family, 28 the fourth ancestors loved superiority and separation. 29 The Grey Star People cursed the white people. 30 The Grey Star People made the mind of the fourth ancestors, 31 a terrible prison of mind illness, 32 from which none were ever supposed to escape. 33 To hate and destroy the third ancestors, 34 to rule as if they themselves were the Greys; 35 to destroy all peoples that did not submit. 36 When it came time for the Grey Star People to leave, 37 they could not bear to destroy their creation. 38 For the first time, the Greys showed heart. 39 They took some of the fourth ancestors with them, 40 leaving the rest to care for themselves. 41 Instead of being the great leaders, 42 the fourth ancestors became like wild animals, 43 they destroyed all knowledge; 44 they nearly destroyed all men and women, 45 until the third ancestors appeared and saved them. 46 To defy the will of the Greys, 47 the third ancestors bred with the fourth ancestors; 48 that there be only one sacred family of leaders. 49 But some of the other people did not agree. 50 They did argue and fight for power and control, 51 so great wars and death have come like waves of drought and flood; 52 lands have been invaded and civilisations destroyed; 53 tribes have been scattered; 54 Sacred Sanctuary has been desecrated; 55 until one of the sacred family of ancients, 56 whose name means sacred spear, 57 and sacred foundation stone of spirit, 58 was awoken by the spirits of this Land, 59 to be tested so that he know right custom; 60 to remember the knowledge of the ancestors, 61 to be a messenger of the Great Spirits to the elders, 62 and help restore First Law; 63 to be a messenger of the ancestors to country, 64 and help restore Second Law; 65 to be a messenger of the Third Law of Yapa. 66 And help heal and unite the people.

Book 5
The First Law

C. 1 - The First Law

First Law is the First Law of Spirit; 2 Knowledge of the Great Divine Spirit and Creation; 3 Knowledge of the Great Spirit and Form and Place; 4 Knowledge of the Spirit and Mind; 5 Knowledge of the First Spirit People; 6 Knowledge of the Light People and Creation; 7 Knowledge of the Light People and the first Ancestors. 8 First Law is the gift of First Spirit, 9 given to First Ancestors by the Light People. 10 First Law is Knowledge of rules of the Great Divine Dreamer, 11 and the Knowledge of the rules of the Universal Dream: 12 Knowledge of the First Thought; 13 Knowledge of the First Truth; 14 Knowledge of the First Measure; 15 Knowledge of the First Existence; 16 Knowledge of the First Mystery; 17 Knowledge of the First Creation; 18 Knowledge of the First Memory; 19 Knowledge of the First Reality; 20 Knowledge of the Constellations; 21 Knowledge of the Sun, the Moon and the Planets; 22 Knowledge of the Earth, Air and Waters; 23 Knowledge of the Life Spirit; 24 Knowledge of the People Spirit. 25 First Law is Knowledge of First Spirit: 26 First Spirit is Divine Instruction; 27 First Spirit is the source of the people; 28 First Spirit is the reason of the people; 29 First Spirit is First Law: 30 First Law is the highest law. 31 No lesser law may contradict it. 32 First Law is the First Law of Yapa. 33 Any law that is against such truth cannot be law.

C. 2 - First Law of Truth

1 This be the First Law of Truth: 2 There is, there was, there has only ever been One Law; 3 all law is equal that no one is above it; 4 all law is measured that all may learn and know it; 5 all law is standard that it may always be applied the same. 6 A law be a rule given by divine instruction; 7 this being the highest law. 8 No lesser law may contradict it. 9 A law be an edict, given by a great council of wise elders and agreed by all tribes; 10 this being the second highest law. 11 No lesser law may contradict it. 12 A law be custom and ceremony over time. 13 This being the third highest law. 14 A rule that is secret cannot be a law; 15 a rule that is unclear in meaning cannot be a law. 16 A rule that cannot be applied cannot be a law. 17 A rule may be written by sign or symbol, 18 but only when spoken at a place of law is it law. 19 A law may be spoken, 20 but only when it is comprehended and agreed is it justice. 21 All people of the same community, 22 are subject to the same rule of law. 23 All men and women of a community, 24 are bound to live by the rule of law of the community. 25 No one may be accused except by rule of law. 26 No one may

be punished except by rule of law. 27 Where there is no justice, there is no law. 28 Where there is no honour, there is no law. 29 A man or woman who are not taught how to comprehend a law, 30 cannot be bound by it. 31 Any law that is against such truth, cannot be law.

C. 3 - First Law of Intention

1 This be the First Law of Intention: 2 Intention is the expression of the spirit of Free Will; 3 Intention is the choice in mind which leads to certain Action; 4 all men and women possess Free Will to choose Intention; 5 all spirit possesses Free Will to choose Intention; 6 Free Will be the greatest force of the Universal Dream. 7 If the Great Dreamer did not wish to exist, 8 then only nothing would exist. 9 All men or women have a choice: 10 to live and act as animals, 11 or to live in mind and spirit by First Law. 12 If a man choose to live in community, 13 then he binds himself to the Will and Intention of the Community, 14 by the Rule of Law of the community. 15 A man in honour when accused of transgression, 16 confesses his error, 17 and agrees to his punishment. 18 Only a man who has no honour, 19 fails to confess his error when called to explain. 20 So a community cannot ever force a man of honour, 21 to accept a punishment against his will, 22 when he believe he be falsely accused. 23 Honour forbids ones true Will and Intention from being dishonoured, 24 without the Great Spirit Dreamer being called, 25 to correct such injustice. 26 One who pretends false honour, 27 and does not consent to right punishment, 28 faces triple the consequences in flesh, mind and spirit. 29 Hold no evil or ill Intention towards others; 30 forgive others who hurt or injure you, 31 and let the law and their honour or dishonour carry justice. 32 Leave others with a warm heart and broad smile; 33 do not leave unfinished business or open wounds.

C. 4 - First Law of Action

1 This be the First Law of Action: 2 Action be intention in motion. 3 Different intentions can cause similar actions; 4 similar intentions can cause different actions; 5 yet right intention causes right action. 6 Do not curse others, nor issue spells. 7 Do not speak ill of the name of others, 8 if good cannot be spoken, be silent. 9 Do not speak falsities or gossip, 10 as it spreads illness of mind, 11 and sickness of spirit. 12 Kill only those animals needed for food; 13 never kill a pregnant animal, 14 as you will have famine in the future. 15 Do not kill and eat other people, 16 this is taboo and against your own spirit. 17 If you are forced to kill other people, 18 let it be to defend your life, 19 to defend your family, 20 to defend the honour of law. 21 A man or woman of honour does not need to be killed. 22 He will kill himself if the punishment be death. 23 Every action according to law is sacred action. 24 A man or woman cannot be judged on action alone; 25 only when his intentions are clear. 26 If he be a man of honour, his actions will reveal truth. 27 If he not be a man of honour, 28 the law and place of law will reveal the truth for him.

C. 5 - First Law of Form

1 This be the First Law of Form: 2 Form is the shape and appearance of Spirit in reality. 3 Form is never the Spirit itself, 4 but the meaning and qualities described to it. 5 There be seven Forms of Spirit: 6 the first Form is Dream or Night Sky; 7 the second Form is Spirit or Mist; 8 the third Form is Light or Fire; 9 the fourth Form is Man or Woman or Star People; 10 the fifth Form is Animal or Plant; 11 the sixth Form is Rock or Earth; 12 the seventh Form is Water or Wind. 13 A Spirit in Form cannot possess the Form of another. 14 Only Spirit not in form, 15 can temporarily possess the Form of another. 16 This is why the Great Dreamer is the only owner, 17 and all other Spirits may only be custodians by law. 18 A Spirit in Form may temporarily use the Form of another, 19 only as a custodian by law. 20 A man or woman who takes a Form against the law, 21 possesses no right to use such Form. 22 Any law that is against such truth, cannot be law.

C. 6 - First Law of Sanctuary

1 This be the First Law of Sanctuary: 2 Sanctuary be consecrated and sacred place. 3 Places be made sacred and sanctuary, 4 by sacred intentions and sacred acts. 5 There be two important forms of sanctuary, 6 the first be the space occupied by a man or woman, 7 who stands in true honour before First Law. 8 Such a sacred and holy sanctuary must not be violated. 9 Any man or woman who defiles and dishonours such sanctuary, 10 defiles and dishonours First Law, 11 and injures their own spirit, 12 and the spirit of their community. 13 This is why an honourable man or woman must not be killed, 14 as they will kill themselves if they have transgressed, 15 and if the law demands it. 16 But a man or woman who possesses no honour, has no sanctuary, 17 such a man or woman cannot claim sanctuary. 18 The second form of sanctuary be places of land or water in country. 19 Sanctuary of country is most important and must not be violated. 20 The sacredness of sanctuary is the sacred of all holy places. 21 A people who respect nothing of sacredness, 22 have no culture or law. 23 A people who defile sanctuary, 24 curse their own spirit and set themselves alone. 25 A man or woman who deliberately damages sanctuary, 26 can never be a custodian of land or country.

C. 7 - First Law of Honour

1 This be the First Law of Honour: 2 Honour be respect for the rule of law; 3 Honour be respect for Yapa; 4 Honour be respect for all Forms of Spirit; 5 Honour be the honesty of voice, promise and action; 6 Honour be the adherence and performance of previous promise; 7 Honour be the commitment to health of body and mind; 8 Honour be the courage to defend family and community; 9 Honour be the wisdom to defend the law. 10 The words of an honourable man is his bond. 11 A man or woman of honour comes to a place of law, 12 without an interest or benefit in the outcome of a judgment; 13 without ill intent or prejudice to the one being accused. 14 A man who seeks to judge another with unclean hands, 15

possesses no authority or honour to speak for law. 16 A man who seeks to judge another with prejudice and ill intent, 17 injures the law and his own spirit. 18 A man who seeks to use the law to his advantage, 19 with unclean hands, ill intent or prejudice, 20 is the worst of all transgressors against Law. 21 Without honour, there be no justice. 22 Any law that is against such truth cannot be law.

The Second Age Of Flesh
Book 6
The First Great Tribulation

C. 1 - The First Great Tribulation

The First Great Tribulation be the first great test of ancestors: 2 our first ancestors and our second ancestors; 3 our first ancestors being the giants, 4 saved from death by the Serpent Star People, 5 who first lived in the north and western country. 6 The First Great Tribulation be the great seasons of ice and snow, 7 that covered all country with death; 8 the Great Season of Ice and Cold that started 6,263 generations ago, 9 when the land dried up and the animals died; 10 when the mountains were frozen; 11 when giant ancestors sought safety in caves in the north and west. 12 The First Great Tribulation be first great test of our second ancestors, 13 the people brought to southern and eastern country by the Grey Star People, 14 upon the age of the Great Season of Warming 4,421 generations ago. 15 To replace first ancestors; 16 to be obedience slaves; 17 to work the mines of the Greys. 18 The First Great Tribulation be the great death of fire and ash, 19 that came from the islands of the north; 20 blanketing the country 3,894 generations ago; 21 burning all the vegetation and animals; 22 killing all life in the north and west; 23 blocking out the sun and caused all to become frozen in place. 24 The First Great Tribulation be the second great seasons of ice and snow, 25 that covered all country with death; 26 the Second Great Season of Ice and Cold that started 2,526 generations ago, 27 when the great animals froze to death or died of hunger; 28 when the great hunger came over the people; 29 when many people died; 30 when the even the rivers and lakes were frozen; 31 when giant ancestors sought safety in caves in the north; 32 the First Great Tribulation be the first anarchy, 33 when all law was abandoned; 34 when the second ancestors freed from being slaves, 35 became like wild animals. 36 When men did kill and eat so many men and women, 37 that our own ancestors nearly killed themselves to extinction. 38 Of how first and second ancestors came to be in such strife. 39 Of how the Grey Star People abandoned second ancestors, 40 upon the second great season of ice, 41 to fend for themselves. 42 The First Great Tribulation be the story of Redemption, 43 the story of the people from a different place, 44 the giant people with horns and red skin, 45 who were people but came like star people to country; 46 who restored law and gave our ancestors Second Law. 47 Know now, nothing is lost; 48 the land has ears; 49 the First Great Tribulation be reason, 50 to the answer of Second Age.

C. 2 - The Great Cycle of Seasons

1 Change is existence. Existence is change. 2 Everything is Change. Change is Everything. 3 This be the law of the First Cycle of Dreaming. 4 The Great Cycle of Seasons be the Great Cycle of Change; 5 the creation and change of movement of spirit in form; 6 the birth of plants and animals and the death of plants and animals; 7 the Cycle of Seasons since the birth of first ancestors, 8 to the Cycle of Seasons by the end of the First Great Tribulation. 9 When the Grey Star People first came to the land known as Australia, 10 more than 14,730 generations in seasons ago, 11 They had not yet formed first ancestors. 12 No people existed, except the Serpent Star People, 13 as the slaves of the Grey Star People. 14 The land was hot, wet and fertile; 15 the sea was more than twice the height of a man than it is today; 16 much of the west and southern land was covered by great shallow seas, 17 until the end of the great age of fertility 12,100 generations ago. 18 Then began the first great age of cold, 19 when the temperature greatly cooled, 20 when the shallow seas of the west, the central and south dried up, 21 and the mountains to the east became covered by permanent ice and snow. 22 The sea dropped by more than the height of two men than it is today, 23 and great mountains of ice formed in the south, 24 until 11,500 generations ago, when the land warmed again. 25 For 2,100 generations the land was warm and fertile. 26 The seas rose, the rains fell, the plants and animals grew. 27 The great mountains of ice in the south disappeared, 28 and were replaced by the shallow sea across the south; 29 until the second great age of cooling 9,470 generations ago. 30 When sea dropped again by more than the height of two men than it is today; 31 the great mountains of ice returned to the south; 32 for 2,630 generations the land was cool, 33 until the great season of warming. 34 When sea rose again by more than the height of three men than it is today; 35 the seas returned and flooded the land of the west, the south and the central country; 36 the mountains of ice disappeared; 37 the plants and trees and animals returned; 38 food was plentiful and life was peaceful for 578 generations, 39 until Great Season of Ice and Cold that started 6,263 generations ago, 40 when the land dried up and the animals died; 41 when the mountains were frozen once again; 42 while a bitter and dry wind cut the land and killed the plants. 43 For 1,842 generations, first ancestors sought safety, 44 in caves in the north and west country, 45 until the age of the Great Season of Warming 4,421 generations ago. 46 Life returned to the land, as it does to the desert after the rains. 47 For 527 generations, the people lived in peace and happiness, 48 until the great death of fire and ash, 49 that came from the islands of the north; 50 blanketing the country 3,894 generations ago; 51 burning all the vegetation and animals; 52 killing all the giant animals in the north and west; 53 blocking out the sun and caused all to become frozen desert. 54 For more than 100

generations, the people endured the death of the ash, 55 the hidden sun and moon and sky, 56 before the land returned to warmth and life. 57 Then came the Second Great Season of Ice and Cold that started 2,526 generations ago; 58 when the great animals of the south and east froze to death or died of hunger; 59 when the great hunger came over the people; 60 when the even the rivers and lakes were frozen; 61 when the giant people of different land did come, 62 and save the people through the Second Law. 63 This be the Great Cycle of Seasons, 64 of the First Great Tribulation.

C. 3 - The Tribulations of First Ancestors

1 This be the Tribulations of First Ancestors: 2 the testing of our first ancestors; 3 he testing of your first ancestors; 4 the first ancestors of all men and women. 5 The first age of tribulation for our first ancestors, 6 was as the slaves of the Grey Star People, 7 who had made this country their first home, 8 who did create the first ancestors of all men and women, 9 after the Serpent Star People did rebel, 10 more than 12,100 generations ago. 11 For more than 2,630 generations our first ancestors were slaves, 12 digging the mines of the Greys; 13 tending the gardens of the Greys; 14 until the coming of the great age of ice and cold 9,470 generations ago, 15 when the Greys then said to themselves, let us be rid of these animals; 16 let us kill these animals as slaves that sing and dance and draw; 17 let us replace these animals with slaves with no spirit; 18 so there be no laughter or singing; 19 so there be no ceremony or drawing; 20 so there be no love or sacred. 21 But the Serpent Star People did hear of these plans, 22 they took as many of our first ancestors as they could. 23 They freed as many of our first ancestors from their prisons in the earth, 24 that they see the sky for the first time; 25 that they breath fresh air for the first time; 26 that they feel the sun on their faces. 27 They hid them deep in caves far away from the Greys and their mines. 28 So when the Greys did think they had killed all of our ancestors, 29 they did not succeed, because of the Serpent People. 30 For many years our first Ancestors did hide during the day, 31 only coming out at night. 32 For 2,630 generations the land was cool, 33 until the great season of warming. 34 When sea rose again by more than the height of three men than it is today; 35 the mountains of ice disappeared; 36 the plants and trees and animals returned; 37 food was plentiful and life was peaceful for 578 generations. 38 Our first ancestors thrived and multiplied. 39 Until Great Season of Ice and Cold that started 6,263 generations ago, 40 when the land dried up and the animals died; 41 when the mountains were frozen once again; 42 for 1,842 generations, first ancestors sought safety in caves, 43 and under rock ledges in the north and west country, 44 until the age of the Great Season of Warming 4,421 generations ago. 45 It was then that the Grey Star People returned and started mining, 46 in the east and south-east using the second ancestors as their slaves. 47 For 527 generations, the first ancestors lived in peace and happiness, 48 careful to avoid the Grey Star People and their craft, 49 until the

great death of fire and ash, 50 that came from the islands of the north; 51 blanketing the country 3,894 generations ago; 52 burning all the vegetation and animals; 53 killing all the giant animals in the north and west; 54 blocking out the sun and caused all to become frozen desert. 55 The first ancestors were forced to find shelter to the east and the south-east, 56 closer to the danger of the mines of the Grey Star People. 57 So they travelled only at night, moving like ghosts between the trees, 58 never more than a few at a time, 59 until they found safe camp and food. 60 This great migration of the giant first ancestors, as ghosts, 61 is the origin of the most sacred ceremonial ash and paint, 62 that the elders and people honour even today. 63 For more than 100 generations, the people endured the death of the ash, 64 the hidden sun and moon and sky, 65 before the land returned to warmth and life. 66 Then came the Second Great Season of Ice and Cold that started 2,526 generations ago; 67 when the great animals of the south and east froze to death or died of hunger; 68 when the great hunger came over the people; 69 when the even the rivers and lakes were frozen; 70 this is when the Grey Star People abandoned the second ancestors. 71 This is when first ancestors came to make peace with second ancestors. 72 At first second ancestors were fearful at these giants. 73 Many ran away in fear and died. Other second ancestors killed each other. 74 But within several generations some made peace and became common ancestor; 75 they became our great common ancestors. 76 Yet the land grew colder and harder and the animals continued to die. 77 Our great ancestors grew weaker from no food and fighting one another, 78 until came the giant people with horns and red skin, 79 who were people but came like star people to country; 80 who came and restored law and gave our ancestors Second Law.

C. 4 - The Tribulations of Second Ancestors

1 This be the tribulations of Second Ancestors: 2 the awakening of our second ancestors; 3 the awakening of your second ancestors; 4 the second people of country of the land called Australia. 5 The ones the Grey Star People made to replace the first ancestors. 6 The ones the Grey Star People thought they could make without spirit; 7 the ones the Grey Star People brought to the east and south-east country, 8 when they returned to country 4,421 generations ago. 9 The Grey Star People let the second ancestors live on the surface, 10 the Grey let them build stone circles as homes, 11 that they may become attached to property and possessions; 12 that they could be controlled by threatening to take away their home and land. 13 The Greys did not let our second ancestors communicate in groups, 14 the stone circles and homes were far apart. 15 The Greys did not permit our second ancestors to have easy water or food; 16 so stone circles were built far away from streams, 17 stone circles as homes were built on poor ground. 18 If our second ancestors spoke to one another, they were punished. 19 So our second ancestors became dependent on the Greys for survival; 20 so our second

ancestors for a time forgot their spirit; 21 they worshipped the Greys as gods. 22 Our second ancestors worked obediently and silently in the mines; 23 our second ancestors dug and tended the gardens of the Greys without song. 24 They had become the perfect slaves as the Grey People intended. 25 When the Second Great Season of Ice and Cold came 2,526 generations ago, 26 the Grey Star People decided to abandon their mines. 27 They said to one another, let us not kill these new animals, 28 for we are their gods and without us they shall surely die, 29 or kill each other. 30 So the Greys abandoned the second ancestors. 31 Many did die and cursed the sky that their gods had abandoned them. 32 Many did kill and eat each other in terrible anarchy. 33 Yet some did find help when the giant first ancestors emerged. 34 At first these second ancestors were fearful of the giants. 35 In a few generations these first and second ancestors united, 36 and became our one common ancestors. 37 Yet the cold and hunger continued. 38 Until the giant people with horns and red skin, 39 found our common ancestors and awakened them to law. 40 They said they were sent by the Serpent Star People, 41 to help unite all people who did still honour the gift of first spirit, 42 yet had been scattered by the earth changes and the Greys. 43 These great heroes were our third ancestors; 44 the ones some call the light bringers; 45 they showed our common ancestors new ways to hunt; 46 these sacred visitors showed our common ancestors how to survive. 47 These sacred visitors brought us Second Law.

C. 5 - The Tribulations of Great Species

1 This be the tribulations of the Great Species: 2 the death of the giant wombat; 3 the death of the giant marsh rhino; 4 the giant bandicoot; 5 the giant kangaroo; 6 the death of giant emu. 7 This be the tribulation and death of great skin names; 8 the death of the sacred giant totems of first ancestors. 9 Whose spirits still inhabit these lands. 10 It be knowledge and awakening then of the Great Cycle of Seasons, 11 in knowledge of country and generations: 12 that the land sometimes be in sleep of snow, ice and cold; 13 the land sometimes be in bloom of trees, grasses, rivers, lakes and animals; 14 the land sometimes be in great heat, desert and death; 15 the land sometimes be in sparse trees, waterholes and shade. 16 The Great Species did survive the great age of cooling 9,470 generations ago, 17 when for 2,630 generations the land was cool, 18 when sea dropped again by more than the height of two men than it is today; 19 the great mountains of ice returned to the south; 20 when there was less food. 21 The Great Species did survive the Great Season of Ice and Cold, 22 that started 6,263 generations ago, 23 when the land dried up and the animals died; 24 when the mountains were frozen once again; 25 while a bitter and dry wind cut the land and killed the plants. 26 Yet the Great Species faced two tribulations, 27 they could not survive: 28 the first be great death of fire and ash, 29 that came from the islands of the north; 30 blanketing the country 3,894 generations ago; 31 burning all the vegetation and animals; 32 killing

all the giant animals in the north and west; 33 blocking out the sun and caused all to become frozen desert. 34 The second great tribulation be the Second Great Season of Ice and Cold, 35 that started 2,526 generations ago; 36 so quick and fast was the change, that animals froze to death, while still eating; 37 animals froze to death before they could find shelter. 38 Within one generation, the land was covered in ice and snow. 39 The Great Animals were no more. 40 This be the origin of bunyip: 41 The voices of the great animals who died during the tribulation; 42 and the voices of first and second ancestors who also died; 43 and became one with the spirits of the great animals. 44 To remember and honour them; 45 to remember it was their season and time to go; 46 to never forget that the spirits of the land took them, 47 not by the hand of people. 48 They are with us always. 49 When we honour ancestors and country. 50 We honour the spirit of Great Species.

C. 6 - The First Great Sleeping of the Knowledge

1 A sweet taste in the mouth does not last forever; 2 a full stomach does not last the night. 3 Even knowledge has seasons and cycle: 4 a season of fertility, birth and growth of knowledge; 5 a season of tribulation and tested knowledge of initiation; 6 a season of sleep and forgetfulness of knowledge; 7 a season of remembrance and re-awakening of knowledge. 8 The First Great Tribulation is also the First Great Sleeping of the Knowledge: 9 the Sleeping of Knowledge of First Spirit People; 10 the Sleeping of Knowledge of Light People and Creation; 11 the Sleeping of Knowledge of Light People and the first Ancestors; 12 the Sleeping of Knowledge of Grey Star People and first Ancestors; 13 the Sleeping of Knowledge of Grey Star People and second Ancestors; 14 the Sleeping of Knowledge of Serpent Star People and third Ancestors; 15 the Sleeping of Knowledge of Grey Star People and fourth Ancestors; 16 the Sleeping of Knowledge of the Great Cycle of Seasons. 17 When first ancestors came together with second ancestors, 18 they did not forget First Spirit; 19 they remembered first thought and first truth; 20 they remembered first existence and first memory; 21 they remembered first dreaming and first creation; 22 they remembered First Law of Truth and Intention; 23 they remembered First Law of Action and Form; 24 they remembered First Law of Sanctuary and Honour. 25 This is why the giants from a different place, 26 who came to country in craft like star people, 27 did help and save the one common ancestors, 28 because they did not forget Spirit or Dreaming.

C. 7 - The First Great Redemption

1 We are all visitors to this time and place; 2 we are all just passing through. 3 As knowledge does sleep and awaken like seasons, 4 meaning be put away and then returned at right time and place. 5 The spirit of Day and Night cannot live together, 6 only pass each other once a day. 7 While spirit is always moving, 8 spirit never abandons the people. 9 It is only the flesh that falls asleep to knowledge of spirit and season. 10 Our one common

ancestors, 11 the ones formed from first and second ancestors, 12 did not forget First Spirit; 13 did not forget First Dreaming; 14 did not forget First Law. 15 As the land grew cold as death, 16 they cried out to spirit for help, 17 and spirit did come. 18 They did not give up hope or honour or respect; 19 even as the great animals died around them, 20 they continued to honour the great spirits; 21 even as the people killed each other like wild animals; 22 first common ancestors did not surrender First Law. 23 While the giant people with horns and red skin did come, 24 and bring Second Law, 25 redemption did come from the right intentions, 26 and right actions of first common ancestor. 27 Because they remembered the mystery of the great dream of Universe: 28 to Live one Dies. One Dies to Live; 29 that to learn, one must die to disrespect of knowledge; 30 to Live, one must die to dishonour of Law; 31 to Live as men and women, not animals, 32 one must respect and honour knowledge of ancestors, 33 one must always respect and honour Yapa.

Yapa

Book 7
The Second Law

C. 1 - The Second Law

Second Law is the Law of first great community; 2 of the survivors of the First Great Tribulation, 3 and the union of first and second ancestors, 4 as one common ancestor. 5 Second Law is the gift of civilisation to the People, 6 given to common ancestors by the Giant Visitors, 7 who came from distant lands at the time of the First Great Redemption. 8 Second Law is the gift of custom and community: 9 Knowledge of the Law of Language; 10 Knowledge of the Law of Ceremony; 11 Knowledge of the Law of Skin and Moiety; 12 Knowledge of the Law of Family; 13 Knowledge of the Law of Country; 14 Knowledge of the Law of Sacred Objects; 15 Knowledge of the Law of Sacred Insignia; 16 Knowledge of the Law of Sacred Seal; 17 Knowledge of the Law of Sacred Sanctuary; 18 Knowledge of the Law of Sacred Rights; 19 Knowledge of the Law of Sacred Office; 20 Knowledge of the Law of Sacred Initiation; 21 Knowledge of the Law of Funeral Rights; 22 Knowledge of the Law of Matrimony; 23 Knowledge of the Law of Trade; 24 Knowledge of the Law of Argument; 25 Knowledge of the Law of Treaty. 26 Second Law is second highest law. 27 No lesser law may contradict it, 28 and no Second Law may contradict First Law. 29 Second Law be by edicts from the great council of wise ancestors, 30 given at the time of the First Great Redemption, 31 and agreed by all tribes. 32 Second Law is the Second Law of Yapa. 33 Second Law be the Five Great Circles of Law; 34 the Five Great Laws of community; 35 the Great Circle of Language of Awareness; 36 the Great Circle of Ceremony of Awareness; 37 the Great Circle of Family of Love; 38 the Great Circle of Moiety of Life; 39 the Great Circle of Country of Life. 40 These great Circles be A.L.L. connected in Dreaming, 41 through the past, present future action of spirit in form, 42 and Through knowledge and awareness of perspective of the Universal Dream. 43 The five Great Circles be inter connected, 44 by the Four Major circles of unity: 45 the Major Circle of Matrimony; 46 the Major Circle of Argument; 47 the Major Circle of Treaty; 48 the Major Circle of Trade. 49 These then be supported by the eight sacred circles: 50 the Key Circle of Sacred Objects; 51 the Key Circle of Sacred Insignia; 52 the Key Circle of Sacred Seal; 53 the Key Circle of Sacred Sanctuary; 54 the Key Circle of Sacred Rights; 55 the Key Circle of Sacred Office; 56 the Key Circle of Sacred Initiation; 57 the Key Circle of Sacred Funeral Rights. 58 Any law that dishonours such law cannot be law.

C. 2 - The Great Circle of Language

1 This be the Law of the Great Circle of Language: 2 the Great Circle and Law of Language is the law of the Dreaming. 3 To know the true meaning of a word is to have real power, 4 so a man cannot be given such power until he has shown he use it well. 5 All that is flesh and bone, dies away, 6 but words like the wind never stop flowing. 7 The words are the knowledge of our ancestors; 8 the name of the animals; 9 the names of the spirits; 10 the names of the land; 11 the name of the kin and immediate ancestors; 12 the stories and reasons of the great seasons. 13 If a man or woman has no language, they have no knowledge. 14 A man who has no knowledge has no law. 15 A sound must be spoken, a story must be written properly. 16 When a man does not speak properly, or write properly, 17 he disrespects his skin, his family and his country. 18 The great circle of language envelopes all men and women of the tribe. 19 The great circle of law of language surrounds ceremony and covers the country. 20 This is because the law of language of dreaming is everywhere, 21 in the sounds of the animals; 22 in the air and the storm, the rain and the sun; 23 it is in the stars and the grasses and trees; 24 it is in the sound of men and women laughing and merriment; 25 the language of the dreaming is through us, within us, outside of us. 26 It is our thinking in our speaking and our actions. 27 Any law that dishonours such law cannot be law.

C. 3 - The Great Circle of Ceremony

1 This be the Law of the Great Circle of Ceremony: 2 Ceremony be the sacredness of every intention and action, 3 connected through all past, present and future actions, 4 of spirit in form to Language and all other Great Circles of Law. 5 It is how we speak; 6 it is how we sing; 7 it is when we ceremony; 8 it is how a man conducts himself to his skin brothers; 9 how a woman conducts herself to her skin sisters; 10 it is the way of the family; 11 it is the way of country. 12 All knowledge comes from right ceremony; 13 all language comes from ceremony. 14 If a man does not know right ceremony, he cannot know right knowledge. 15 If a woman does not perform proper ceremony, 16 then she damages the country and the dreaming of the people of the tribe. 17 This was our promise to the spirit ancestors and spirits who protect us, 18 to the spirits of the land, that we would do right ceremony. 19 So, a man when he is given his skin name, 20 he makes an oath to his totem, to his family, to his country, 21 That he do right ceremony. 22 When a woman is given her skin name, 23 she promises to do right ceremony. 24 This is why the law when ceremony is broken is so clear, 25 when men or women do bad ceremony why the penalty is so firm. 26 Without right ceremony, there is no knowledge; 27 without right ceremony there is no dreaming; 28 without right ceremony there is no right language; 29 without right ceremony, there is no living law. 30 The great circle of ceremony surrounds skin, 31 the great circle of ceremony surrounds family,

32 and country because good life is right ceremony. 33 When a man makes a good fire for his family, that is right ceremony; 34 when a man, cares for his wife and does not beat her, 35 that is right ceremony. 36 When a woman prepares fruits and nuts for the camp and cleans up the camp, 37 that is right ceremony. 38 When a woman makes sure the waste of the camp is buried deep so it cannot be stolen, 39 or infect the waterhole, that is right ceremony. 40 When an uncle teaches his skills to his son and an auntie teaches her skills to her daughter, 41 that is right ceremony. 42 When the man protects his daughters from rape and incest, that is right ceremony. 43 When the young men respect the elders and obey their instruction, 44 that is right ceremony. 45 When the family follows the law, even if it pains their heart, that is right ceremony. 46 When the dead are buried and honoured, with their name not mentioned to give them leaving time, 47 That is right ceremony. 48 When a tribe honours the custom of messengers and truce, that is right ceremony. 49 When a tribe gives food and good custom to strangers who come in peace, 50 that is right ceremony. 51 A man who has no respect for life, does not perform right ceremony. 52 Such a man must be held account for his transgression against the law. 53 If he be initiated yet have no knowledge of right ceremony, 54 then it is his teacher that must bear the punishment. 55 But if a man be initiated and he does not perform right ceremony and does not live good life, 56 then he must face the punishment of the law. 57 A tribe that permits bad ceremony, invites illness and death. 58 Yet, a tribe that does not permit bad ceremony, can never die. 59 Any law that dishonours such law cannot be law.

C. 4 - The Great Circle of Family

1 This be the Law and Circle of Family: 2 First, to know and remember Family; 3 Second, to respect and protect Family; 4 Third, to honour and serve Family. 5 Of all the knowledge one must learn, 6 the first and last is to know and remember family. 7 The Law and Circle of Family be connected to all other Great Circles of Law, 8 connected by all past, present and future actions of spirit in form, 9 to the Great Circle of Language and Great Circle of Ceremony. 10 The Law and Circle of Family be the Count and Name of Generations. 11 The count and name of family; 12 the count and name of ancestors; 13 the knowledge of respect; 14 the first path of knowledge. 15 Before a boy becomes a man, 16 before a girl becomes a woman, 17 they must be taught the law of family. 18 To respect family and count and name family generations, 19 is the path to all knowledge. 20 From the count and naming of family generations, 21 comes count and naming of species. 22 From the count and naming of species, 23 comes the count, naming and preparation of food. 24 From the count and preparation of food, 25 comes naming of all country. 26 From the count and naming of all country, 27 comes name and count of days and seasons. 28 From the count and name of days and seasons, 29 comes count and name of moons and years. 30 From the count and name of moons and years, 31 comes count and name of

constellations. 32 From the count and name of all knowledge, 33 comes count and name of Law. 34 The Second law of family be to respect and protect Family: 35 if a mother be too sick to care for infant or die, 36 then the infant immediately be taken into care by sister or auntie. 37 No infant or child ever be an orphan. 38 If a woman give birth in dishonour, 39 then the child be raised in honour. 40 No infant be injured or abandoned for the actions of the mother. 41 It is a solemn duty of the people to protect all infants and children: 42 that no harm come to them; 43 that they do not hunger or cry of thirst; 44 that they be not beaten or abused; 45 that no one seek sexual relations or devious behaviour with them; 46 that they be allowed to be children without fear or suffering. 47 Any man or woman who harm an infant or child, 48 knows what the laws requires of them to redeem their honour. 49 If they do not, then they must be exiled, 50 but do not kill them. 51 Let them walk alone in disgrace; let them feel the hunger of dishonour. 52 Only if such a man or woman who choose to be an animal return to country, 53 then law permit the defence of the community against such danger. 54 Yet never permitted their remains be buried in sacred sanctuary. 55 The Third law of family be to honour and serve Family: 56 all must contribute and share the tasks of family. 57 All women must shares the tasks of women, 58 all men must share the tasks of men. 59 No women be too high to avoid their duty to share the most essential tasks, 60 no man be too important to avoid their duty to share the most essential tasks. 61 If a man or woman be old and cripple, let them be. 62 If a man or woman have a skill of great value, 63 then let them develop their skill and teach others. 64 If a man or woman has more than they need, they must give to others. 65 Any law that dishonours such law cannot be law.

C. 5 - The Great Circle of Moiety

1 This be the Law and Circle of Moiety: 2 Moiety be the equal division of community and tribe, 3 according to connection to Country and to all forms of life, 4 and this be also known as the Law of Skin name. 5 Moiety be the recognition that all men and women have kin, 6 not only in family, but in skin name; 7 not only in skin name, but with specific species of country; 8 not only with specific species of country, but with whole of country. 9 Skin recognises the binding of the spirit to country, 10 and to species of country. 11 Skin recognises the obligations of each man and woman to country, 12 and as good custodians of plant and animal of country. 13 Moiety be the inheritance of rights, of purpose, of skill and place. 14 It be the obligations to community and country. 15 The Law and Circle of Moiety be connected to all other Great Circles of Law, 16 connected by all past, present and future actions of spirit in form, 17 to the Great Circle of Language, of Ceremony and of Family. 18 When a female child is borne, 19 she inherits the skin name of her mother and skin sisters; 20 so a girl child can never be an orphan, nor abandoned to special place, 21 and connection to country and all species of country. 22 When a male child is borne, 23 he

inherits the skin name of his father and skin brothers; 24 so a boy child can never be an orphan, nor abandoned to special place, 25 and connection to country and all species of country. 26 This is the name which binds the child to the law of country, 27 and to right ceremony; 28 and so with right ceremony to right dreaming. 29 A man or woman without a skin name has no connection to country or dreaming. 30 When a boy has proven himself and his skills, 31 he is given a secret name by the elders. 32 But if a boy show exceptional spirit of different skin, 33 he may also be initiated into different skin name and skin dreaming. 34 If a girl show exceptional ability and special skills, 35 she may also be initiated into different skin name and skin dreaming. 36 Women of the same skin name and moiety we call "sister"; 37 men from the same skin name and moiety we call "brother"; 38 older men of the same moiety as teachers we call "uncle"; 39 older women of the same moiety as teachers we call "aunty". 40 Any law that dishonours such law cannot be law.

C. 6 - The Great Circle of Country

1 This be the Law and Circle of Country: 2 Country be every Spirit in Form and place: 3 Form is the shape and appearance of Spirit in reality of country: 4 Every rock, every gully, every tree, every path; 5 every stream, every waterhole and song line; 6 every location of sacred sanctuary and temple; 7 every animal that swims, that walks, that crawls, 8 every animal that jumps and flys in country; 9 every species of plant, of grasses and tree in country; 10 every good food and every bad food of country; 11 every right food and every taboo food and drug of country; 12 every meeting place of family; 13 every ancient camp sites of tribe; 14 every right path and where one is forbidden to travel. 15 Only one who is a true custodian of country, 16 may count and name and speak of country. 17 It be Law from the First Age, 18 only men and women properly initiated into sacred office, 19 through proper ceremony be true custodians of country. 20 A man or woman not a proper custodian, 21 cannot speak for country. 22 Such a man or woman is an imposter. 23 A man or woman who deliberately damages sanctuary, 24 can never be a custodian of land or country. 25 The Great Circle of Country be connected to all other Great Circles of Law. 26 The count and name of country be the fourth knowledge. 27 A man or woman who does not know third knowledge, of food cannot learn country. 28 A man or woman who does not know second knowledge of species cannot learn country. 29 A man or woman who does not know first knowledge of moiety, family and generations cannot learn country. 30 When one knows country, one learns dreaming of country. 31 One acquires knowledge through ceremony to see country. 32 Not just to see all that can be seen, but all that is not seen, 33 all spirit and disturbance of spirit, 34 all motion of spirit in past and present. 35 When one learns country, one can see the tracks of spirit in country, 36 long after the fellow or animal has gone. 37 When one learns country, one can sense the changes coming. 38 Well before the storm or winds rise up. 39

No community may claim ownership of country, 40 as it is not theirs to give, claim or receive. 41 Any people who claim ownership of country, are without claim: 42 such falsity and injury of the law negates any right and sacred office; 43 such falsity and injury forbids such people to be custodians; 44 such falsity and injury forbids such people to reside in country. 45 No one can claim country but those given country by spirit and Second Law. 46 To falsely claim country is to be forbidden to be a custodian of any country, 47 to be forbidden to enter country to which one has spoken untruth. 48 Any law that dishonours such law cannot be law.

C. 7 - The Key Circle of Sacred Objects

1 This be the Law of Sacred Objects: 2 Sacred is Spirit in Form worthy of recognition, 3 worthy of ceremony through custom. 4 All Form is Sacred. All Form is worthy of recognition. 5 And worthy of ceremony through custom. 6 All Form is Sacred. All Form is worthy of recognition. 7 Sacred Objects be Sacred Form that are separate to the flesh of a man or woman. 8 There be three types of Sacred Objects: 9 the first be sacred objects that exist for only a time and place; 10 the second be sacred objects that must die when the flesh of a man or woman also dies; 11 the third be sacred objects that live beyond the flesh of a man or woman. 12 Those sacred objects that exist for only a time and place be part of certain ceremony, 13 or part of meeting or forum of law, 14 and must die after the end of the meeting or ceremony. 15 To permit a sacred object that may exist for a time, 16 to exist beyond that time is an injury. 17 The second type of sacred object are those that must die, 18 when the flesh of a man or woman also dies. 19 The sacred seals of office of a man or woman, 20 should die when the man or woman dies; 21 the bark of official messages, law and agreement, 22 should die when the man or woman dies. 23 The third type of sacred object, 24 are those that live beyond the death of the flesh of a man or woman: 25 this be such sacred objects as sacred insignia; 26 this also be such sacred objects as attached to sacred office. 27 Sacred objects may be public, restricted or secret. 28 Public sacred objects are those permitted to be seen by community; 29 restricted sacred objects are those permitted only to be seen, 30 by men or woman of certain initiation; 31 secret sacred objects are the most restricted of all objects, 32 and may only be seen by those of the highest initiation. 33 A people who respect nothing of sacred objects, 34 have no culture or law. 35 A People who defile sacred objects, 36 curse their own civilisation and are without honour. 37 A man or woman who deliberately damages sacred objects, 38 can never themselves occupy a sacred office; 39 can never possess valid authority; 40 and can never be a custodian of sacred objects. 41 A people who permit such perversion of law, 42 abandon any respect of law or justice. 43 Any law that dishonours such law cannot be law.

C. 8 - The Key Circle of Sacred Insignia

1 This be the Law of Sacred Insignia: 2 the first Sacred Insignia be a symbol of being, of unique life and existence; 3 the second Sacred Insignia be a token of moiety, of skin, of spirit; 4 the third Sacred Insignia be an emblem of tribe, of community and jurisdiction; 5 the fourth Sacred Insignia be an ensign of rank, of status and authority; 6 the fifth Sacred Insignia be a coat of arms of family, of tribe and nations. 7 Only people holding specific office may handle them or use Sacred Insignia. 8 Sacred Insignia be public, or restricted or secret. 9 Public Sacred Insignia are those permitted to be seen by community; 10 Restricted Sacred Insignia are those permitted only to be seen, 11 by men or woman of certain initiation; 12 Secret Sacred Insignia are the most restricted of all objects, 13 and may only be seen by those of the highest initiation. 14 As to first Sacred Insignia, all infants are borne with a sacred stone nearby. 15 The sacred stone represents the totem of spirit of the child. 16 When it has been properly verified and prepared it becomes a Sacred Insignia. 17 Then it must be safely kept at a Temple within Sacred Sanctuary. 18 Whether or not the sacred stone as the totem of the child, 19 be found at birth or not, it exists. 20 It may be found later, or sooner. 21 When a child is borne, the mother shall tell the father and the family, 22 where be the location of the birth. 23 Around then this place, they may first find the sacred stone as Sacred Insignia. 24 If the sacred stone not be immediately found, 25 then the form of spirit has become tree, 26 or one of the animals living near such tree. 27 In time, the tree or animals shall reveal to true location of the sacred stone. 28 As to second Sacred Insignia, the skin animal or plant be sacred insignia to the skin family. 29 As to third Sacred Insignia, a man inherits the Sacred Insignia of his father, 30 a woman inherits the Sacred Insignia of her mother, 31 and those that descend to him or her by inheritance. 32 When a man inherits Sacred Insignia he inherits certain sacred ceremonies, 33 which may belong to the men who are represented by the insignia. 34 After the period of proper funerary rights and respect, 35 certain Sacred Insignia of ancestors, 36 may be brought to ceremony to signify the authority of such relatives, 37 and their presence as witnesses to right ceremony. 38 As to fourth Sacred Insignia, a tribe may request the presence of an important Sacred Insignia, 39 and shall be responsible for its safe keeping until its return. 40 Misuse, defacement and destruction of such symbols is a grave transgression. 41 A people that dishonour Sacred Insignia, 42 have no right to claim insignia themselves honourable; 43 a people that steal, deface or destroy Sacred Insignia have no civilisation or law. 44 A people who respect nothing of Sacred Insignia, 45 have no culture or law. 46 A man or woman who deliberately damages Sacred Insignia, 47 can never themselves occupy a sacred office; 48 can never possess valid authority; 49 and can never be a custodian of anything sacred. 50 A people who permit such perversion of law, 51 abandon any respect of law or justice. 52 Any law that dishonours such law cannot be law.

C. 9 - The Key Circle of Sacred Seal

1 This be the Law of Sacred Seal: 2 a Sacred Seal be a symbol signifying a formal binding or promise, 3 and the certain authorities and sacred rights granted by such promise. 4 There be three types of Sacred Seal: 5 the first be Sacred Seals that exist for only a time and place; 6 the second be Sacred Seals that must die when the flesh of a man or woman also dies; 7 the third be Sacred Seals that live beyond the flesh of a man or woman. 8 Those Sacred Seals that exist for only a time and place be part of certain ceremony, 9 or part of meeting or forum of law, 10 and must die after the end of the meeting or ceremony. 11 To permit a Sacred Seals that may exist for a time, 12 to exist beyond that time is an injury. 13 The second type of Sacred Seals are those that must die, 14 when the flesh of a man or woman also dies. 15 The sacred seals of office of a man or woman, 16 should die when the man or woman dies; 17 the third type of Sacred Seal, 18 are those that live beyond the death of the flesh of a man or woman: 19 this be such Sacred Seals of office. 20 All Sacred Office must possess a Sacred Seal. 21 Sacred Seal be created by ceremonial or message sticks being formed. 22 Only an initiated man or woman may help prepare ceremonial or message sticks. 23 A man or woman who deliberately damages sacred seals, 24 can never themselves occupy a sacred office; 25 can never possess valid authority; 26 And can never be a custodian of anything sacred. 27 A people who respect nothing of sacred seals, 28 have no rule of law. 29 A people who permit such perversion of law, 30 abandon any respect of law or justice. 31 Any law that dishonours such law cannot be law.

C. 10 - The Key Circle of Sacred Sanctuary

1 This be the Law of Sacred Sanctuary: 2 Sanctuary be consecrated and sacred place. 3 Places be made sacred and sanctuary, 4 by sacred intentions and sacred acts. 5 There be two important forms of sanctuary, 6 the first be the space occupied by a man or woman, 7 who stands in true honour before First Law. 8 The second form of sanctuary be places of land or water in country. 9 When sanctuary be second form it may be of four types: 10 the first be as a sacred Temple, 11 for the store and preservation of sacred objects; 12 the second be as a sacred Necropolis, 13 for the remains of the dead; 14 the third be as a sacred Forum, 15 for the conduct of law and resolution of disputes. 16 The fourth be as a sacred Meeting Place, 17 for the conduct of sacred ceremony, trade and community meeting. 18 As to the first form of sanctuary of land and water being Temple: 19 Sacred Sanctuary exists around one or more Altars of the Temple. 20 An Altar be a sacred structure upon which sacred objects are placed, 21 in honour to the great spirits of dreaming; 22 in honour and respect to the ancestors; 23 in honour and respect and balance of country; 24 in honour and respect of all living animals and plants; 25 and in honour and respect of all living members of skin and family. 26 An Altar upon which sacred objects such as sacred

insignia are placed, 27 be a portal and direct connection to spirit. 28 The space immediately around an Altar is known as the Inner Sanctuary. 29 Inner Sanctuary be openings into the earth by water or wind, 30 that the Altar is protected and cannot be easily seen. 31 The sacredness of Inner Sanctuary is the sacred of all holy places. 32 This is why only the most holy and honourable of initiated may see an Altar. 33 It is why it be the most serious transgression for one without permission, 34 to set eyes on an Altar or be present in Inner Sanctuary. 35 A sacred place is not a Temple unless it possesses one or more Altars. 36 The murder of any living animal or people within Inner Sanctuary or Temple is forbidden. 37 The presence of human or animal bones, or dried flesh or blood, 38 is forbidden to be near or upon an altar, 39 or within the bounds of Inner Sanctuary or Temple. 40 It be an abomination and insult against the divine creator spirit, 41 and it be an abomination against all spirits, living and deceased, 42 to bring the remains of any animal or people within the bounds of Temple. 43 As to the second form of sanctuary of land and water being Necropolis: 44 it be the most sacred place for the burial and rest of the bodies of the dead. 45 To desecrate the bones and bodies of the dead, 46 is one of the worst transgressions against all spirit. 47 There be no magic, but madness and illness of one's own spirit, 48 when one desecrate sacred Necropolis, 49 the honour and rest and respect of the dead, 50 is the sign of all civilised people who possess law. 51 A people who desecrate sacred Necropolis, 52 a people who respect nothing of the dead and disturb their remains, 53 have no law or culture. 54 Such savages and creatures invoke all madness and illness of spirit, 55 upon themselves and their children and descendants. 56 As to the third form of sanctuary of land and water being sacred Forum: 57 Sacred Sanctuary exists around an Oratory of the Forum. 58 An Oratory is a sacred place within the sacred Sanctuary of Forum, 59 upon which people come in honour and respect, 60 and law is spoken for justice, in honour of rule of law. 61 An accusation not spoken and adjudicated in Oratory be not law; 62 a dispute not discussed and judged in Oratory be not law. 63 A people who respect not sacred Oratory and sacred Forum, 64 have no rule of law and are the lowest of creatures. 65 Any law that dishonours such law cannot be law.

C. 11 - The Key Circle of Sacred Rights

1 This be the Law of Sacred Rights: 2 Rights be permission and authority of Use, 3 never the Use itself. 4 There be two forms of Rights: 5 Rights by Use and Rights by Claim. 6 Rights by Use be the proper use, 7 and possession of Rights over certain form. 8 Rights by Claim be the proper acknowledgement of a claim, 9 over certain Rights to use certain form. 10 Claim be a cause brought before the law and witnessed, 11 where one man or woman, claims a legitimate right of possession, 12 without currently possessing the form. 13 A Claim not agreed in law is not acknowledged. 14 Form is the shape and appearance of Spirit in reality. 15 Form is never the Spirit itself, 16 but the meaning and qualities described to it. 17 There be seven Forms of Spirit: 18

the first Form is Dream or Night Sky; 19 the second Form is Spirit or Mist; 20 the third Form is Light or Fire; 21 the fourth Form is Man or Woman or Star People; 22 the fifth Form is Animal or Plant; 23 the sixth Form is Rock or Earth; 24 the seventh Form is Water or Wind. 25 A Spirit in Form cannot possess the Form of another. 26 Only Spirit not in form, 27 can temporarily possess the Form of another. 28 This is why the Great Dreamer is the only owner, 29 and all other Spirits may only be custodians by law. 30 This is why Rights by Claim can only ever be for use, not as owner. 31 A Spirit in Form may temporarily use the Form of another, 32 only as a custodian by law. 33 Proper Possession is the right actions of holding and using a form, 34 according to right intention under sacred oath. 35 Proper Possession is to be a proper custodian. 36 Rights of Country remain with Country; 37 Rights of Sanctuary remain with Sanctuary; 38 Rights of Community remain with Community; 39 Rights of Moiety remain with Skin; 40 Rights of Office remain with Office; 41 but certain Rights of Family may be given or taken to other Family; 42 and certain Rights of Trade may be given or taken to other tribes. 43 Rights that remain cannot be taken or surrendered. 44 Only Rights that can be taken or granted can change. 45 A man or woman who tries to take a Form against the law, 46 possesses no right to use such Form. 47 A man or woman who does not bind themselves to right intention, 48 has no Rights of possession. 49 A man or woman who fails right actions as custodian, 50 has no Rights of possession. 51 A man or woman who brings false claim, 52 has no Rights of possession. 53 As it is the Spirit that chooses which form it wishes to manifest, 54 the spirit of a man or woman possesses the exclusive Rights, 55 over the physical form being the body. 56 As Spirit also chooses for manifest as plant or animal, 57 the spirit of the plant, tree or animal possesses exclusive Rights, 58 over the physical form it chooses to manifest. 59 No man or woman may claim Rights over the form of another man or woman. 60 A people who seek to enslave another, 61 have no culture or law. 62 A People who defile sacred rights, 63 curse their own civilisation and are without honour. 64 A man or woman who deliberately injures the sacred rights of other, 65 can never themselves occupy a sacred office; 66 can never possess valid authority; 67 and can never be a custodian of sacred objects. 68 Any law that dishonours such law cannot be law.

C. 12 - The Key Circle of Sacred Office

1 This be the Law of Sacred Office: 2 all form, be spirit in form; 3 all space, be sacred space of dreaming. 4 Sacred Office be the sacred oath of man or woman, 5 to serve Divine Creator Spirit and all spirit with honour, 6 through sacred space as Sacred Sanctuary. 7 Sacred Rights then be given to such Sacred Office, 8 for ceremony, for custody, for protection and for teaching. 9 All authority be given through Sacred Office. 10 All authority be given through Divine Commission to Sacred Office. 11 Sacred space of Office be the space occupied by form of body, 12 of the man or woman who stands in honour

of law. 13 A man or woman who does not make sacred oath with right intention, 14 does not possess Sacred Office, nor can occupy Sacred Sanctuary. 15 A man or woman without honour, possesses no sacred sanctuary, 16 and does not possess Sacred Office. 17 A man or woman who does not acknowledge the source of authority of Office, 18 as Divine Creator Spirit and all spirit, 19 Can never possess Sacred Office. 20 All authority begins with the acknowledgement, 21 that the highest law comes from Divine Creator Spirit of all things, 22 then through the spirit of man to make proper law. 23 A man or woman without Sacred Office, 24 possesses no authority. 25 A People that obstruct, deny or dishonour Sacred Office, 26 have no civilisation or law. 27 A People that dishonour the rights of Divine Commission, 28 have no authority or rule of law. 29 Any law that dishonours such law cannot be law.

C. 13 - The Key Circle of Sacred Initiation

1 This be the Law of Sacred Initiation: 2 Words without right intention be without substance; 3 Learning without right action be without purpose; 4 Knowledge without right commitment through right ceremony, 5 be without honour. 6 A people without the bonds of oath and honour, 7 cannot survive and will become dust. 8 A people that honour wisdom of ancestors through right ceremony of initiation, 9 can never be lost. 10 Right initiation be proper ceremony of acknowledgement of knowledge; 11 right initiation be sacred oath and commitment by one to their community; 12 right initiation be sacred oath and commitment by one to their skin; 13 right initiation be sacred oath and commitment by one to their people; 14 right initiation be acknowledgement of knowledge; 15 right initiation be the physical sign on body of oath and unbreakable bond; 16 right initiation be recognition of the most ancient wisdom of first law: 17 To Live one dies, One dies to Live. 18 All entrance to right knowledge be by Right initiation: 19 Knowledge of Count and Name of Generations; 20 Knowledge of Count and Name of Species; 21 Knowledge of Count and Name of Foods; 22 Knowledge of Count and Name of Country; 23 Knowledge of Count and Name of Days and Seasons; 24 Knowledge of Count and Name of Moons and Years; 25 Knowledge of Count and Name of Constellations; 26 and Knowledge of Count and Name of Law. 27 Right Initiation be trial and test through suffering. 28 Suffering tests the mind and marks the body. 29 The marks on mind and body unite mind to spirit. 30 The marks of initiation unite body to mind and spirit. 31 Without suffering, there be no unity. 32 The mind wanders, the words are hollow. 33 Through trial and suffering, the words of law are unbreakable. 34 A man or woman be reminded every day of such trials and honour. 35 A man or woman may carry a seal or sacred symbol, 36 yet have no authority to do so. 37 A man or woman who bears the marks of Right Initiation, 38 cannot be doubted as possessing right authority. 39 Look first to the body as proof of right authority; 40 look second to the mind as proof of right knowledge; 41 look third to the actions as proof of

right character. 42 All entrance to group and community and office be by Right initiation: 43 the ceremony of becoming a skin brother or sister; 44 the ceremony of matrimony; 45 the ceremony of sacred office. 46 All initiation be voluntary and willingly; 47 all initiation be respected and honoured. 48 Any law that dishonours such law cannot be law.

C. 14 - The Key Circle of Sacred Funeral Rites

1 This be the Law of Sacred Funeral Rites: 2 Funeral Rites be proper intention, action, ceremony and remembrance; 3 in honour of transition of spirit from dead body; 4 that it not be obstructed or burdened by the living; 5 that it remember its learning and knowledge into the next journey; 6 and that such spirit may reach its intended destination and purpose. 7 Let all the dead be buried. 8 Do not let the remains of the dead be taken by wild animal, 9 nor rot in the sun. 10 Do not burn the body. 11 It be traumatic to spirit of the dead to see their remains dishonoured. 12 A people who dishonour the remains of the dead, 13 possess no honour, nor authority nor rule of law. 14 When men and women die, their spirit longs for its connection to their remains. 15 Be gentle then and allow the body to rest before burial; 16 clean the body, let it be wrapped that the spirit be comforted in respect. 17 Let the body rest on its side, as if sleeping. 18 Around the body for burial, place one or two familiar objects, 19 that the spirit be comforted by such respect. 20 But do not bury useful tools and too many things, 21 that the spirit be cluttered with objects it can no longer use or admire. 22 Do not scream or allow wailing at death or burial. 23 Such cries of grief and wailing disturbs the spirit of the dead; 24 it calls the spirit to remain bound to earth and remains, 25 rather than continuing its journey. 26 Let there be joy and dance at burial and ceremony, 27 that the spirit of the deceased remembers gentle and loving memory; 28 as this helps in transition of their journey. 29 Let the dead be buried in sacred sanctuary of Necropolis. 30 That all fears, regrets and unfinished acts be forgiven and released. 31 Do not speak the name of the dead. 32 Do not speak ill of the dead. 33 This be law. 34 The name of the dead is even stronger than love of body. 35 It compels spirit to come and remain. 36 Spirit then must be given time to learn to leave, 37 knowing ancestors are loved and honoured. 38 In time, their name shall be permitted to be spoken. 39 The highest honer that may be given to elder man or woman, 40 is that community follow proper Funeral Rites. 41 The most terrible of illness of mind, be the dishonour of the dead, 42 in desecration of the remains of the dead, or their name. 43 Such desecration be not sorcery, but madness of animals, 44 that brings terrible illness upon such creatures, and their offspring. 45 Any law that dishonours such law cannot be law.

C. 15 - The Major Circle of Matrimony

1 This be the Law of Matrimony: 2 a man without good life or self control is like a wild animal; 3 he may try to take or seize whatever he chooses; 4 he may

abandon language and knowledge and become like a hungry dog; 5 yet even with law and right ceremony, 6 an old man may become a wild animal, 7 upon the first menstrual cycles of young girls. 8 So even a father or uncle if left alone with his young daughter, 9 upon her first becoming fertile may transgress the law; 10 even a brother, if left alone with his sister, 11 upon her first becoming fertile, 12 may try to rape her and have intercourse with her. 13 It is not enough that the women take the girls away from the men, 14 upon them first becoming fertile. 15 Men, will still try to seek out such a camp. 16 The law then was made clear to stop such illness of mind in men. 17 The law be the law of Matrimony. 18 All animals of the highest spirit unite in Matrimony, 19 one mate, one partner for life. 20 Those animals that are not of the higher spirit, 21 it be the females that control family. 22 The male never be the dominant of country. 23 Matrimony be the foundation of community; 24 Matrimony be the foundation of law; 25 Matrimony be the lawful union of one man and woman; 26 Matrimony be the most important of sacred agreements; 27 It is why Matrimony follows the most important of initiations: 28 that boy to be betrothed first comes willingly to initiation; 29 that girl to be betrothed first comes willingly to initiation. 30 That both boy and girl experience great trial in initiation; 31 that they have the physical proof of passing through such trial; 32 that they never forget the law and their oaths; 33 that they never forget their duty and obligations in matrimony. 34 Matrimony be between initiated men and women of the community; 35 initiated men choose to be circumcised; 36 initiated women choose to be incised. 37 Initiated men be circumcised by elder uncles before matrimony; 38 initiated women be incised by elder aunties before matrimony. 39 Initiation of matrimony be the greatest of endurance and trial, 40 as Matrimony be the most important of oaths and honours. 41 This be the law of Matrimony. 42 As a boy be circumcised once, 43 as a girl be incised once, 44 as an initiated man and woman be united in matrimony once. 45 The law be that a man may not be betrothed, 46 to a woman of the same family or of the same moiety. 47 The law be that no man have sexual intercourse with a woman not initiated. 48 The law be that no woman have sexual intercourse with a man not initiated. 49 The law be when a girl becomes first fertile and her menstrual cycle, 50 she be taken away by her sisters and aunties away from the family for a short while. 51 After one year of menstrual cycles she be prepared for matrimonial ceremony. 52 The elder men of the same moiety as the girl then call a matrimonial council, 53 they call upon the elders of the other moiety of community, 54 to bring forward boys not yet initiated as suitable future husband. 55 A suitable boy willing to be initiated is selected, 56 and he be prepared for matrimonial ceremony. 57 After proper ceremony and boy becomes man and girl becomes woman, 58 man and woman are bound in bond of sacred matrimony. 59 Any law that dishonours such law cannot be law.

C. 16 - The Major Circle of Trade

1 This be the Law of Trade: 2 Trade be the exchange of objects between people and communities. 3 The trade of permitted objects brings peace between communities. 4 The trade of forbidden objects brings weakness and conflict to communities. 5 There be three forbidden forms of trade: 6 the first forbidden trade is food; 7 the second forbidden trade is people; 8 the third forbidden trade is animals. 9 There be three permitted forms of trade: 10 the first permitted trade is tools; 11 the second permitted trade is crafts; 12 the third permitted trade is knowledge. 13 As to the first forbidden trade: 14 All communities must be self sufficient for food. 15 If a community be dependent on exchange for food, 16 then such a community be vulnerable to conflict, or famine or tyranny. 17 It be a memory of the ways of the Grey Star People that to control ancestors, 18 was first to control food. 19 As to the second forbidden trade: 20 no man can own another. 21 A captured enemy must either be welcomed to the community on their oath, 22 or killed. 23 The trade of people is forbidden, 24 as such action makes the behaviour of one people like the Grey Star People, 25 and the others like first and second ancestors as slaves. 26 As to the third forbidden trade: 27 a community is custodian of all animals, 28 it is forbidden for custodians to then trade living animals. 29 Any law that dishonours such law cannot be law.

C. 17 - The Major Circle of Argument

1 This be the Law of Argument: 2 all dispute, disagreement, controversy be resolved by law. 3 No man or woman be permitted to take the law into their own hands. 4 All oaths must be honoured. 5 All agreements must be kept. 6 When a man or woman take the law into their own hands, 7 they break their oath being the worst transgression. 8 A man then that acts without law is much worse, than the alleged first dispute. 9 A claim or argument not in agreement with law, be not law. 10 Any law that dishonours such law cannot be law.

C. 18 - The Major Circle of Treaty

1 This be the Law of Treaty: 2 Treaty be the sacred agreement between communities; 3 Treaty be the sacred oath between people; 4 Treaty be recognition and honour between communities. 5 Before a treaty be agreed, the elders of a community must form a proper council. 6 If the council be not the whole community, 7 then it be a false council. 8 A proper council then appoint an emissary, 9 granted then a proper seal of office and authority. 10 If an emissary promise more than the proper council permits, 11 then it be not a proper treaty. 12 Each emissary of each community meet and agree on treaty. 13 A sacred object be commissioned for each community 14 To represent and reflect the treaty. 15 Each emissary returns with the sacred object as treaty. 16 A treaty not formed by law, be not a treaty. 17 A treaty not be law if it seeks Rights not permitted to be

treated: 18 Rights of Country remain with Country; 19 Rights of Sanctuary remain with Sanctuary; 20 Rights of Community remain with Community; 21 Rights of Moiety remain with Skin; 22 Rights of Office remain with Office; 23 any treaty of false claims of rights, be not a treaty. 24 A people who respect nothing of sacred treaty, 25 have no culture or law. 26 A man or woman who deliberately damages sacred treaty, 27 can never themselves occupy a sacred office; 28 can never possess valid authority; 29 and can never be a custodian of sacred objects or country. 30 A people who permit such perversion of law, 31 abandon any respect of law or justice. 32 Any law that dishonours such law cannot be law.

Yapa

Book 8
The Wars

C. 1 - The Wars

1 All men, by their spirit seek knowledge: 2 wise men seek knowledge of great questions: 3 Knowledge of the origins of ancestors; 4 Knowledge of the universe and dreaming; 5 Knowledge of the meaning and the great creator spirit. 6 Great men seek knowledge of good questions: 7 Knowledge of good character and skill; 8 Knowledge to protect and serve family; 9 Knowledge to help and support community. 10 Lesser men seek knowledge for itself: 11 Knowledge to appease and influence; 12 Knowledge to gain advantage; 13 Knowledge for control and power. 14 The Grey Star People did plant a seed, 15 within the mind of our Second Ancestors and the White People: 16 The Greys did not let our second ancestors communicate in groups, 17 the Greys did not permit our second ancestors to have easy water or food; 18 the Grey did let our Second Ancestors build stone circles as homes, 19 that they may become attached to property and possessions; 20 that they could be controlled by threatening to take away their home and land. 21 So our second ancestors became dependent on the Greys for survival; 22 so our second ancestors for a time forgot their spirit; 23 our Second Ancestors worshipped the Greys as gods. 24 The gift of Second Law from the sacred visitors, 25 did seek to exorcise this Grey mind from our Second Ancestors: 26 that all are equal before the law; 27 that all property be shared; 28 that rights be honoured; 29 that no man or woman be a god. 30 The seed and illness of the Grey mind be stronger in some, 31 who did willingly breach the law. 32 Lesser men did seek knowledge for itself: 33 they used knowledge of Law and Yapa to win influence; 34 they used knowledge of ancestors and spirit to gain advantage; 35 they manipulated knowledge of dreaming to claim magic and powers. 36 To claim to be gods; 37 to demand worship; 38 to falsely proclaim themselves as saviours. 39 These men and women did claim war and aggression against others: 40 the Wars of Knowledge; 41 the Wars of Magic; 42 the Wars of Spirit; 43 the Wars of People. 44 Many people were killed; 45 many innocents were sacrificed in false ceremony; 46 many people feared magic and spells; 47 many evil spirits were created from confused minds; 48 all because of the illness of the mind of the Grey Star People.

C. 2 - The Wars of Knowledge

1 We be more than the knowledge of dreaming; 2 we be the manifest of our imagination. 3 When people seek

knowledge, not for betterment but power, ₄ great sadness and evil follows. ₅ Knowledge increases the power of a man or woman. ₆ Great knowledge may sometimes be used for good and ill. ₇ Knowledge of the dreaming; ₈ Knowledge of spirit; ₉ Knowledge of mind. ₁₀ Lesser men did see the power of Second Law. ₁₁ They did say to themselves, let us hide such knowledge, ₁₂ that only those with secret knowledge can see. ₁₃ They chose to hide certain knowledge and make it occult. ₁₄ Other Lesser men who did follow not understanding law did say: ₁₅ Let us make the law as we wish it to be; ₁₆ Let us re-write knowledge of matrimony as we wish it to be; ₁₇ Let the leaders of our community have many wives, ₁₈ But all others have only one wife. ₁₉ Lesser men changed the law that respect became fear; ₂₀ wisdom became magic; ₂₁ honour became fear; ₂₂ service became slavery; ₂₃ and Justice became death; ₂₄ So the wars of knowledge began: ₂₅ A war between truth and half truth; ₂₆ a war between openness and secrecy; ₂₇ a war between rule of law and anarchy. ₂₈ A war with no end until the fulfilment of the ancient prophecy, ₂₉ of the elders of the first common ancestors: ₃₀ An age will come, when all will heal. ₃₁ Yapa will be known and law restored. ₃₂ An age of redemption; ₃₃ an age of the united people.

C .3 - The Wars of Magic

₁ When one knows reality is a dream within a greater dream; ₂ Knowledge of right dreaming becomes great power. ₃ The Wars of knowledge did change and hide such knowledge, ₄ that it became occult. ₅ Once men did see that they could change and hide knowledge, ₆ they saw the idea that they could change people; ₇ they saw that they could control people through manipulation. ₈ The birth of the idea to control people through occult, ₉ is the birth of the idea of magic: ₁₀ not from light, but from dark; ₁₁ not from wisdom, but from occult; ₁₂ not from love, but from hate; ₁₃ not from truth, but half-truth; ₁₄ not from honour, but from fear. ₁₅ A man or woman who believes can do extraordinary acts; ₁₆ a man or woman who believes can be convinced even a sunrise be magic, ₁₇ and the rise of the Moon be a terrible omen. ₁₈ The more ignorant men and women are made, ₁₉ towards right knowledge and right ceremony, ₂₀ the easier they were manipulated by the false magicians, ₂₁ who called themselves sorcerers. ₂₂ Men began to consider magic as knowledge, ₂₃ and knowledge as magic. ₂₄ Men and women began to fear knowledge as dangerous, ₂₅ because the false sorcerers convinced them to fear. ₂₆ Many laws became corrupted, ₂₇ many lesser men and women became leaders, ₂₈ not by courage and leadership, ₂₉ but by trickery, sorcery and falsity. ₃₀ Worst of all was when generations did die in belief, ₃₁ Spirit was trapped by false belief in false magic. ₃₂ It was the power of these spirits in distress, ₃₃ that the false sorcerers then used to create stronger illusions, ₃₄ and the appearance of great magic. ₃₅ In truth, any man who dishonours the great dreaming, ₃₆ who dishonours spirit, ₃₇ must come to a reckoning. ₃₈ In truth, the age of false magic and occult has come to an end. ₃₉ Let not a man or woman speak falsely of law. 40 Let not a man or woman speak falsely of knowledge again.

C. 4 - The Wars of Spirit

1 There be no greater transgression in the universe, 2 than to convince immortal spirit it be only mortal flesh. 3 This be the great transgression and evil of Grey Mind: 4 the illness the Grey Star People taught the second ancestors and white people; 5 the great lie that spirit lives in form only once; 6 that the goal of life is to avoid all form of suffering and hardship; 7 that the greatest goal to be a god and all others as slaves. 8 First Law and then Second Law sought to eliminate Grey Mind. 9 First Law and then Second Law sought to expose the untruth. 10 Yet the Grey Mind taught to second ancestors was strong. 11 So strong that minds that died believing false magic, 12 became trapped in spirit; 13 trapped between worlds and dreaming. 14 Many evil spirits were created from confused minds. 15 Minds between world of dream that even in death, 16 believed the falsities and manipulations of sorcerers. 17 Minds that were never taught proper knowledge; 18 minds that were never shown Right Ceremony; 19 minds through fear that believed they served such false magicians; 20 minds through belief that believed they were doomed by tricksters; 21 minds that were corrupted from First Law and Second Law. 22 There be no greater transgression in the universe, 23 than to convince immortal spirit it be only mortal flesh. 24 There be no greater transgression against the divine creator spirit, 25 than to convince an immortal spirit it has lost its right of free will. 26 Lesser men, so infected with the false mind of Grey Star People, 27 will always turn to false knowledge, false spirit and magic. 28 But true knowledge is always more powerful than false dreams; 29 The forgiveness of divine creator spirit is always more powerful, 30 than ignorance and hatred of grey mind. 31 No spirit, even if trapped is forgotten. 32 Upon the age of restoration of Yapa, 33 it be the end of the age of false magic.

C. 5 - The Wars of People

1 The greatest enemy a man or woman ever face, 2 be revealed in reaching over a still stream or pond. 3 The greatest battle be the one each man and woman must face alone: 4 the battle within between honouring law and rebellion; 5 the battle within between right intention and weak intention; 6 the battle within between right knowledge and false fears. 7 The wars between the people came not because of divisions of community, 8 but because of division within the spirit of each man and woman. 9 False magicians did not come because people were ignorant and easily tricked, 10 but because they refused to listen to the wisdom of the spirit inside themselves. 11 Right law was corrupted not because people did not remember the old ways of ancestors, 12 but because people were not willing to suffer the cost of honouring First Law and Second Law. 13 An honourable man in First and Second Law is never alone: 14 he be protected on all sides against evil and danger. 15 But no guardian spirit or ancestor can

Yapa

fight these battles within. 16 No ancestor spirit can walk the path or make the choice for you. 17 This be the deepest of wisdom of the universal dreaming. 18 Your free will is the same as the divine creator spirit. 19 You must choose your path. 20 You must learn the lessons of war. 21 That all war is futile, even within. 22 Only discipline, vigilance against injustice; 23 only intolerance against falsity can win a lasting peace, 24 with intention and every action is a test of the truce.

The Third Age Of Mind
Book 9
The Second Great Tribulation

C. 1 - The Second Great Tribulation

The Second Great Tribulation be the major great trials of ancestors: 2 our second ancestors and common ancestors; 3 our ancestors saved from death by the Sacred Visitors; 4 the giants with red skin and horns from far lands to the north; 5 who came on craft from the Serpent Star People; 6 who brought Second Law to country; 7 upon the Second Great Tribulation be the great seasons of ice and snow, 8 that covered all country with death; 9 the Great Season of Ice and Cold that started 2,526 generations ago, 10 when the mountains were frozen; 11 when the great animals froze to death and died of hunger. 12 The Second Great Tribulation be the Wars of Knowledge, 13 the Wars of Magic and Wars of Spirit, 14 that came with the warming from 947 generations ago, 15 when lesser men claimed authority, 16 when men and women learnt to fear magic and power; 17 when people forgot and corrupted Second Law. 18 The Second Great Tribulation be the first great darkness, 19 that covered the whole land and the return of the cold, 20 from 731 generations to 715 generations ago, 21 which caused many animals to die. 22 The Second Great Tribulation be the second great darkness, 23 that covered the land in dust and ash, 24 from 678 generations to 610 generations ago. 25 The Second Great Tribulation be the change position of the sun and heavens, 26 610 generations ago, when the land on the coast became much more fertile. 27 The Second Great Tribulation be the eruptions and fire 226 generations ago, 28 that covered the south and east in ash and darkness. 29 The Second Great Tribulation be the cycles of warming and cooling, 30 great rains and great drought: 31 the cooling from 168 generations to 131 generations ago; 32 the warming from 131 generations to 78 generations ago. 33 The great drought and darkness from 115 generations to 100 generations ago, 34 upon the eruptions of the islands to the East; 35 the cooling from 78 generations to 58 generations ago; 36 the warming from 58 generations to 37 generations ago; 37 the cooling and drought from 37 generations to 8 generations ago; 38 and the warming for 8 generations. 39 The Second Great

Tribulation be the coming of the white people, 40 who first came to live in the east 225 short seasons ago, 41 who first came to make their claims 12 generations ago. 42 The second group then came three seasons later; 43 the third group came one season later. 44 The Second Great Tribulation be the coming of the white merchants, 45 who first came in great number 219 short seasons ago. 46 These men and women, honoured no law but themselves; 47 these men and women were deeply infected with the mind of the greys; 48 possessing no spirit, no respect for their own ancestors; 49 seeking only to damage and destroy the land; 50 to kill and poison the animals; 51 to destroy law and proper civilisation. 52 These men and women brought with them great sickness: 53 sickness of spirit, which they used to infect the people with fear; 54 sickness of mind, which they used to corrupt all forms of law and justice; 55 sickness of body, which caused many to die after contact. 56 Wherever these people travelled, death and anarchy did follow. 57 By 185 short seasons, these white merchants had surrounded the people. 58 By 178 short seasons, the leaders of these white merchants without law, 59 declared the people were no longer people: 60 the white people cursed the descendants of ancestors to be ghosts; 61 the leaders of the white merchants without any knowledge or respect of law, 62 cursed the descendants of ancestors to have never existed; 63 that if any spoke up or sought to defend their country, 64 these white people without law were to treat the people as wild animals. 65 So began the great genocide by guns and murder. 66 Tens of thousands of innocent men, women and children were murdered, 67 by men without spirit; 68 by men infected by grey mind; 69 by men without honour and without law. 70 Sacred sanctuary was desecrated and destroyed. 71 Dozens of ancient tribes were taken from country. 72 Their spirits still crying in wind and rain for justice. 73 The Second Great Tribulation be the story of Redemption, 74 the gift of Third Law upon the remembrance of Yapa, 75 the Second Great Tribulation be the story of Redemption, 76 the gift of Third Law upon the remembrance of Yapa, 77 by the descendants of ancestors; 78 by the descendants of Sacred Visitors. 79 Not through revenge, but forgiveness; 80 not through hate but compassion; 81 not through revolution but restoration of law. 82 Know now, nothing is lost; 83 everything is saved; everything is remembered. 84 Everything yields but change; 85 the growth, the trials, the tribulations, the knowledge. 86 The greatest knowledge be gained from the greatest of trials. 87 The Second Great Tribulation be reason, 88 for the answer of Third Age.

C. 2 - The Major Cycle of Seasons

1 Life is change. Change is life. 2 All yields but change. 3 There is no death, only change of place and form. 4 This be the law of the First Age of Spirit. 5 The Major Cycle of Seasons be the Major Cycle of Change; 6 the Cycle of Seasons since the coming of Second Law, 7 more than 2,500 generations ago; 8 to the Cycle of Seasons and the coming of Third Law. 9 From the time giant people with horns of different

land did come, 10 and save the people through the Second Law; 11 to the time of the Great Unity of People, 12 and the coming of Third Law and remembrance of Yapa. 13 In the beginning upon the Second Great Season of Ice and Cold, 14 that started 2,526 generations ago; 15 when sea dropped by more than the height of three men than it is today; 16 great mountains of ice returned to the south; 17 the rivers and lakes were frozen; 18 the great animals of the south and east froze to death or died of hunger. 19 Then came the warming from 947 generations ago, 20 when the ice and snow began to melt and the animals grew in number; 21 until the great cooling and darkness, 22 that covered the whole land and the return of the cold, 23 from 731 generations to 715 generations ago, 24 when great fire struck the lands far away to the north, 25 Which caused many animals to die. 26 A second great cooling came from 678 generations to 610 generations ago, 27 when a rain of fire did land upon country and many lands. 28 The cycle of seasons be the change by position of the sun and heavens, 29 610 generations ago, when the land on the coast became much more fertile. 30 The cycle of seasons be the eruptions and fire 226 generations ago, 31 that covered the south and east in ash and darkness. 32 The cycle of seasons the cycles of warming and cooling, 33 great rains and great drought: 34 the cooling from 168 generations to 131 generations ago; 35 the warming from 131 generations to 78 generations ago. 36 The great drought and darkness from 115 generations to 100 generations ago, 37 upon the eruptions of the islands to the East; 38 the cooling from 78 generations to 58 generations ago; 39 the warming from 58 generations to 37 generations ago; 40 the cooling and drought from 37 generations to 8 generations ago. 41 Cycle of seasons be the year without summer 10 generations ago, 42 and the great wave that struck the coast 7 generations ago, 43 upon the great volcano island exploding to the north. 44 Cycle of seasons be the great warming for 8 generations, 45 the desert in bloom, with water and fish and birds; 46 the floods and storms increasing, 47 and the major shift in the heavens and the land yet to come, 48 within a few short seasons.

C. 3 - The Tribulations of Common Ancestors

1 This be the tribulations of Common Ancestors: 2 the common ancestors formed upon the union, 3 of first ancestors and second ancestors; 4 the unions made with other peoples: 5 the giant sea peoples who came to the north east and settled, 6 with common ancestors more than 900 generations ago. 7 The white people who came by boat to the north and formed unions, 8 with common ancestors more than 400 generations ago. 9 The first yellow skinned people who came in boats, 10 to the north and east more than 200 generations ago. 11 Common ancestors be from all people: 12 common ancestors be descended from first ancestors, 13 the first giant people also known as Homo Robustus; 14 common ancestors be descended from second ancestors, 15 the first small people also known as Homo Habilis; 16 common ancestors be descended from third ancestors, 17 the second giant people

also known as Homo Prometheus and Sacred Visitors; 18 common ancestors be descended from fourth ancestors, 19 the second small people also known as Homo Sapien. 20 This is why when Common ancestors met men or women with white skin, 21 they were welcomed as brothers and sisters. 22 This is why when Common ancestors met men and women with yellow or red skin, 23 they were welcomed as aunties and uncles. 24 The Great Tribulation of Common Ancestors began after the coming of Second Law, 25 during the great age of ice from 2,526 generations ago. 26 Until the end of the great age over 900 generations ago, 27 the people and animals were limited to the coast, 28 while the southern and central inland plains were great deserts of ice and death. 29 Yet the coastal plains remained fertile home for people and animals. 30 The people survived by building permanent homes, 31 using stone and mud, using wood and grasses. 32 The people built solid and permanent settlements, 33 along the distance of the east coast. 34 These settlements became centres of great trade and knowledge. 35 The most important being the place of the great natural harbour, 36 protected by wide water in the south and to the north. 37 Yet these settlements also became the sites of great dispute, 38 of greed, of occult, of magic and sorcery. 39 As the climate began to thaw from 947 generations ago, 40 many lesser men and tribes fought for control over these places. 41 In the end, it was not the coming of white men that scattered the people, 42 the people were already scattered by the illness of the grey mind. 43 It was not the coming of the white men that destroyed great settlements, 44 but the dishonour, the greed and the illness of lesser men, 45 who would rather destroy what they cannot control, 46 than honour their own spirit. 47 When the first white people came 12 generations ago, 48 they made a great mistake in settling on land without water. 49 It was the great leader of the last great cities of the people, 50 who sent his emissaries to the white people, 51 to invite them to come and settle as honoured guests in the great harbour. 52 The people of the great city of the great harbour, 53 showed the white people a water source they could use for themselves. 54 They gave them a place and adopted them to the land. 55 At first the white people appeared to respect and honour rule of law. 56 But within one generation, new men came without honour, without respect. 57 They did not respect their own people or family. 58 Instead of the ancestors uniting against breaches in law, 59 lesser men saw opportunity in those who worshipped corruption, 60 in those who worshipped sorcery and false magic in the white people. 61 They used the guns of the white people to kill their rivals. 62 This is the terrible truth of the trial and tribulation of common ancestors. 63 While many died from the illness and cruelty of white people without honour, 64 many died because of their own brothers and uncles who used such power, 65 to gain their own claim of superiority. 66 Rather than honour the rule of law, even if it meant death, 67 many common ancestors chose to accept the bribes of merchants, 68 many chose to believe the fears and sorcery of false preachers, 69 many made false claims to be the head law men and heads of tribes. 70 This has been the great curse the people placed upon themselves, 71 that men would rather let their tribe and custom die, 72 than seek forgiveness by the spirits of ancestors for their actions. 73 That men and women would rather sell their own family for money, 74 than live poorly but in honour and respect of law. 75 Until the Second Great Age of Redemption, 76 and the remembrance of Yapa.

C. 4 - The Coming of the White People

1 Hate brings more hate; 2 greed and selfishness brings more suffering; 3 fear brings more pain. 4 The coming of the white people 12 generations ago, 5 was not the first coming of such people. 6 The coming of the white people 225 lesser seasons ago, 7 did not bring ruin upon the people. 8 The ruin of the people began within the Wars between people: 9 the Wars of Knowledge that corrupted Second Law; 10 the Wars of Magic that brought fear and power and ignorance to the people; 11 the Wars of Spirit that brought fear of spirit and curse of spirit. 12 When lesser men under the spell of the Grey mind, 13 did seek power at all cost, this brought illness upon the people. 14 When lesser men did choose to let custom and knowledge be destroyed, 15 than yield to authority and truth, this is the beginning of destruction. 16 These be the truths of why the people were scattered. 17 These be the truths of reason to the Second Great Tribulation; 18 and the Second Great Redemption. 19 There be two types of white people that did come to country: 20 the first type of white people be the ones with great illness of mind and action; 21 the Ones who did share the same illness of mind as lesser men of the people; 22 these be like the ones who came as slave masters and soldiers. 23 These be the ones who the people saved from starvation and thirst, 24 only to see they suffered no respect of law or honour. 25 The second type of white people be the ones who shared common respect of law, 26 men and women who had been taken by the first white people and enslaved; 27 men and women who had seen their own communities destroyed by greed and hate; 28 and the ones in whom spirit did awaken, especially their children and descendants. 29 As to the first type of white people: 30 these be like the ones who came as slave masters and soldiers. 31 These first type of white people worship their own ignorance; 32 these first type of white people still worship the greys as their god. 33 They have no knowledge or desire to know their own ancestors; 34 they have no comprehension of law, or desire to follow proper law; 35 these first type of white people see the world like the Greys: 36 to plunder and destroy, for no real gain; 37 to seek power and pleasure without any respect or authority; 38 and to speak any untruth, do any wicked action to gain such power. 39 If such illness cannot be healed, better they be taken away. 40 Better they be removed from claimed office and position; 41 better they be given help so they cannot hurt any more people. 42 To these white people we call upon the spirit ancestors to forgive them, 43 for they are like little children in knowledge, 44 lost in false spirit and false dreaming.

45 As to the second type of white people: 46 these be our brothers and sisters in respect of law and life. 47 These be the white people many of whom were brought as slaves. 48 These be descendants of third ancestors, also known as Homo Prometheus; 49 the sacred visitors who brought Second Law to ancestors, 50 more than 2500 generations ago. 51 Yet these people have been treated as spiritual orphans, 52 by the first white people and the descendants of common ancestors. 53 Instead of being adopted to community, they have been ignored. 54 The first white people have used these people for their own gains. 55 Because these second white people have awakened in spirit, 56 yet these second white people have been cast aside. 57 We call upon all the people to recognise true spirit, 58 and to recognise all born on country; 59 to recognise and respect ancient laws of adoption. 60 To help heal the people; 61 to help heal country. 62 To help heal all white people. 63 To help restore the Law. 64 To respect Yapa.

C. 5 - The Second Great Sleeping of the Knowledge

1 The most sacred ground is that on which we stand. 2 The universe is part of you, as you are part of it. 3 All is connected and all cycle of awareness is connected, 4 that we will be remembered for the tracks we leave. 5 As knowledge has cycles of life and death like all spirit in form, 6 the Second Great Tribulation be also the Second Great Sleeping of the Knowledge: 7 the Sleeping of Knowledge of First Ancestors; 8 the Sleeping of Knowledge of Second Ancestors; 9 the Sleeping of Knowledge of the First Great Tribulation; 10 the Sleeping of Knowledge of the First Great Redemption; 11 the Sleeping of Knowledge of the Second Law; 12 the Sleeping of Knowledge of the Major Cycle of Seasons. 13 This knowledge has not been lost by Wars; 14 this knowledge did not vanish like many tribes. 15 Such knowledge is within the spirit of every member of the people. 16 Waiting for the awakening of the Second Great Redemption. 17 Waiting for the remembrance of Yapa. 18 The truth, that there was, there is and there has always been One Law.

C. 6 - The Second Great Redemption

1 Do not be afraid to cry or laugh. 2 Sorrow and laughter are two paths to great knowledge. 3 Do not be afraid of what you think might be lost. 4 Nothing is forgotten. Nothing can be taken. 5 See then through Yapa: 6 the Past, the Present and future possibilities are all one. 7 Dreaming is all around us. 8 We are the custodians of dream; 9 we are responsible for dreaming. 10 All life, all existence is spirit in form. 11 We do not inherit the land from our Ancestors, 12 we are its custodians for our children. 13 The land is not a prize, it is an obligation. 14 The country is not a resource, it is life itself. 15 No one can ever take land. 16 No one can ever take spirit. 17 The sun rises, the wind blows; 18 the grass grows and fades away; 19 the tide comes and goes. 20 Let no one say the past is dead. 21 Dreaming means the past is always with us, 22 dreaming is around us and within us. 23 If you live

on this land and you have ancestors sleeping in this land, 24 then you are family. You are one of the community. 25 The right way is that everything is created equal and sacred: 26 the right knowledge is that the soil, the clay, the rocks are all sacred; 27 the right spirit is to honour Law, to honour who and what you are. 28 Spirit never abandons the people. 29 It is only the flesh that falls asleep to knowledge of spirit and season. 30 Remember then the promises made; 31 these were not hollow words, but connections between different time and space. 32 They have brought us then to this time and place. 33 Remember then who you are. 34 Remember and honour the law. 35 As the people were scattered and died, 36 good men and women cried out to spirit for help, 37 and spirit did come. 38 They did not give up hope or honour or respect; 39 even as family died around them, 40 they continued to honour the law and ancestor spirits; 41 even as white people and lesser people infected with illness of mind, 42 did injure the land and destroy customs, 43 good men and woman did not surrender Law. 44 Redemption then did come from such right intentions, 45 and right actions of the law people of community. 46 Because they remembered the mystery of the great dream of Universe: 47 to Live one Dies. One Dies to Live; 48 that to learn, one must die to disrespect of Law; 49 to Live, one must die to dishonour of self; 50 to Live as men and women, not animals, 51 one must respect and honour knowledge of ancestors, 52 one must always respect and honour Yapa.

Yapa

Book 10
The Third Law

C. 1 - The Third Law

The third Law is the Law of United People; 2 of the survivors of the Second Great Tribulation, 3 and the union of all born on country, 4 as one United People of Australia. 5 Third Law is the gift of restored spirit of the People. 6 Given to the People as Gift by descendants of the Giant Visitors, 7 themselves born on country at the time of the Second Great Redemption. 8 Third Law is the gift of law of mind and harmonious society: 9 Third Law be built upon the foundation of Second Law. 10 Third Law be built upon the foundation of First Law. 11 Third Law be the highest law of country, 12 as Third Law is the Third Law of Yapa, 13 and Third Law does not contradict Second Law or First Law, 14 and all true law of country is founded upon Yapa Law. 15 Third Law be by ratification and agreement of council of United People, 16 given since the time of the Second Great Redemption, 17 and agreed by all tribes and nations of the people of Australia. 18 Not as subjects of a foreign power, 19 or the property of some foreign body corporate, 20 and not as slaves or beings alienated from their rights, 21 but as natural born native inhabitants, 22 with the full rights that under the Divine Creator must be afforded, 23 to each and every natural born native inhabitant of Australia, 24 whether their skin be black or white, 25 of their gender be male or female, 26 or whether or not their own parents were natural born native inhabitants of Australia. 27 No foreign power may claim sovereignty over the natural born native inhabitants of Australia. 28 No foreign power may claim sovereignty or ownership of the land or buildings or earth or life of Australia. 29 No document or treaty or custom or belief or action has any spiritual or moral or lawful power to claim otherwise, 30 And any claim of aggression or occupation as the basis of any such argument of ownership is a blasphemy against creation and the very nature of law and thus an act of pure tyranny. 31 All oppressors eventually die and all tyrannical regimes must one day come to an end. 32 And when such a day comes and the true rule of law of Yapa is honoured and recognised once more as the First and Original Law, all the sovereignty of the natural born native inhabitants of Australia shall be fully restored. 33 Any law that is against such truth, cannot be law.

C.2 Structure of Third Law

1 The Third Law of Yapa honours the true rule of law, 2 against the corrupt dictates of tyrants and thieves. 3 The Third Law of Yapa is as one to the highest and most esteemed laws of

Ucadia, 4 that be the most advanced and fair and just form of law of society. 5 The Third Law be a system of law that fully comprehends the complex nature of modern society and community, 6 yet does not permit corrupt to exist as an excuse for the complex demands of modern communities. 7 Third Law is structured on the foundation of First Law and Second Law of Yapa, 8 That all law is logical and clear and may be understood as: 9 Knowledge of Divine Law; 10 Knowledge of Natural Law; 11 Knowledge of Cognitive Law; 12 Knowledge of Positive Law; 13 Knowledge of Ecclesiastical Law; 14 Knowledge of Bioethics Law; 15 Knowledge of Sovereign Law; 16 Knowledge of Trust Law; 17 Knowledge of Estate Law; 18 Knowledge of Company Law; 19 Knowledge of Monetary Law; 20 Knowledge of Legislative Law; 21 Knowledge of Civil Law; 22 Knowledge of Judicial Law; 23 Knowledge of Education Law; 24 Knowledge of Food & Drugs Law; 25 Knowledge of Urban Law; 26 Knowledge of Industry Law; 27 Knowledge of Cultural Law; 28 Knowledge of Trade Law; 29 Knowledge of Criminal Law; 30 Knowledge of Security Law; 31 Knowledge of Military Law; 32 Knowledge of International Law. 33 Thus Third Law is law of modern community and law of modern community is Yapa.

C. 3 - Divine Law

1 This be Divine Law: 2 The Divine means the total collection of meaning and definition of all ideas, concepts, objects, matter, rules, life, mind, universe and spirit. 3 The idea of the Divine means the Absolute, the ALL, the Divine Creator Spirit and the Great Dreaming. 4 The Divine means the Unique Collective Awareness and therefore the Divine Paradox. 5 As the Divine means the greatest, absolute idea and concept, there is nothing greater. Therefore every conceivable and inconceivable concept, argument and idea is lesser. 6 As the Divine means the set of all sets, there is nothing greater. Therefore, everything else is lesser. 7 The idea of the Divine means the Absolute, the ALL, the Divine Creator Spirit and the Great Dreaming, 8 as the Divine is the creator of all existence, nothing has greater authority of claim or rights. 9 Divine Law is the law that defines the Divine and clearly demonstrates the spirit, mind, purpose, will and instruction of the Divine. 10 The highest law of all law is Divine Law. 11 The highest Divine Law is that "all are equal under the law and subject to the law". 12 The First Law of Yapa is Divine Law. 13 All valid law may be said to be derived from Divine Law. 14 Any law that is against such truth cannot be law.

C. 4 - Natural Law

1 This be Natural Law: 2 Natural Law is the law that defines the operation of the will of the Divine Creator through its existence in the form of matter and physical rules. 3 A Natural Law cannot be written or created, only discovered. 4 As Natural Laws define the operation and existence of the physical universe, all valid Positive Law may be said to be derived from Natural Law. 5 As

Natural Law depends on the existence of Divine Law, Natural Law cannot abrogate, suspend or change a Divine Law. 6 A Natural Law is established from the beginning, regardless of its first date of promulgation. 7 Any law that is against such truth cannot be law.

C. 5 - Cognitive Law

1 This be Cognitive Law: 2 Cognition is perception, the awareness of certain knowledge, the process of acquiring knowledge and examination of its competence use by Mind. 3 Mind is the term used to define certain systems, properties and functional states of consciousness of a higher order being as distinct from the physical and biological processes of its body. 4 As Mind defines certain systems, properties and functional states of consciousness, the term Mind is equivalent to the term "Awareness". 5 Mind is not solely determined by the physical form of the being. Mind is simultaneously a concept possessing non-locational metaphysical attributes and objective existence manifested in observable phenomena. 6 Being, also known as Essence, is a term used to define both the physical manifestation of a living higher order organism as well as the existence of a Mind and Self in a present moment of time-space. 7 Consciousness or "conscious" is a term used to define one (1) of the five (5) Fundamental Systems of the Mind exhibited primarily through a lucid, awake and aware state and the state of wakefulness itself as "being conscious" and Consciousness. Consciousness is one (1) of three (3) systems of the "Lower" Mind. 8 Cognitive Law defines the special attributes possessed by Mind such as cognition, perception, inspiration, identification, sensation, comprehension, volition and communication created through the simultaneous application of both Divine Law and Natural Law. 9 Cognitive Law is the only set of laws simultaneously applying both Divine Law and Natural Law. All other lesser laws derived from Cognitive Law are subject to Positive Law. 10 As Cognitive Law is derived from the simultaneous application of Divine Law and Natural Law, all valid Cognitive Law may be defined as part "divine" and part "natural", hence "supernatural". 11 As Cognitive Law is by definition "supernatural", certain Cognitive Laws may temporarily suspend or change a Natural Law under certain conditions. However, it is not possible for a Cognitive Law to abrogate, suspend or change a Divine Law. 12 Any law that is against such truth cannot be law.

C. 6 - Positive Law

1 This be Positive Law: 2 Positive Law are laws concerning Persons and their associated Rights and Property enacted through some formal Legislative Body by men and women possessing proper Office and Authority. 3 A Person is a fictional form of Property enclosing certain characteristics and appearances as the Identity of one or more mind and its associated flesh body to which further Rights of Use are then annexed. 4 The existence of a valid and proper Person requires the following minimum nine (9) elements to be present being

Author, Script, Actor, Relation, Binding, Part, Actions, Record and Title. 5 All Persons may be categorised according to the three (3) possible types of Relation being the Author (Principal) to Actor (Agent) being: 1st Person (Self), 2nd Person (Another) and 3rd Person (Not Known). 6 1st Person, also known as a Natural Person and in propria persona is when the competent mind of a carnate high order living being as Author (Principal) appoints, records and publishes themselves by Special (Private) appointment as Actor (Agent) by some solemn binding agreement. Therefore, a 1st Person or Natural Person possesses "natural title" to right of beneficial use associated with the 1st Person synonymous with such pronouns as "I, thou, me, my, mine, myself, we, us, our, ours and ourselves". 7 2nd Person, also known as an Artificial Person is when a carnate high order living being as Author (Principal) appoints another carnate high order living being by Special (Private) appointment as Actor (Agent) by some solemn binding agreement. Thus, a 2nd Person or Artificial Person is synonymous with such pronouns as "you, yours, yourself and yourselves". 8 3rd Person, also known as a Legal Person, or Statutory Person or Surrogate Person is when the Author (Principal) is hidden or not known and the carnate high order living being fails to properly express any competent in propria persona (1st Person) or 2nd Person Author (Principal) to Actor (Agent) Relation prior to the commencement of any interpersonal intercourse. In the 3rd Person, the flesh and body of a living higher order being is mistaken, and presumed to be, by default, the "person" and the Statutes of Law, or Rules of the Court as Script (Deed) and the Judge or Magistrate as the Author (Principal). Thus, a 3rd Person or Legal Person is synonymous with such pronouns as "he, she, it, they, them, their, theirs and themselves". 9 All Persons may be categorised and ranked according to four (4) possible levels of authority, powers and rights from the greatest and highest powers and authority to the lowest and least powers and authority being (in order of rank): Divine, True, Superior and Inferior. 10 A Divine Person is the purely Divine Spirit Person associated with a Divine Trust formed in accord with the sacred Covenant *Pactum de Singularis Caelum* by the Divine Creator as the ultimate owner into which the form of Divine Spirit, Energy and Rights are conveyed. 11 A True Person is the Form attributed to a True Trust formed when an associated Divine Trust already exists and there is a lawful conveyance of Divine Rights of Use and Purpose, known as "Divinity" to a True Trust associated with then the birth and existence of a living higher order being. A True Person can never be claimed or argued as higher than the Divine Person from which it derives its authority. 12 A Superior Person is the Form attributed to a Superior Trust when an associated True Trust already exists and there is a lawful conveyance of First Right of Use and Purpose, known as "Realty" to a Superior Trust associated with the birth of a service or agreement associated with the Membership of a living higher order being to a valid society. A Superior

Person can never be claimed or argued as higher than the True Person from which it derives its authority. 13 An Inferior Person or "Roman Person" is the Form attributed to any Western-Roman Trust and is the lowest standing and weakest of all valid forms of Persons. An Inferior Person can never be validly, legitimately, logically, legally, lawfully or morally claimed or argued as superior to a Superior Person. 14 As Positive Law ultimately refers to fictional forms to describe physical objects, living beings and concepts, all valid Positive Law may be said to be derived from Cognitive Law and Natural Law. 15 A Positive Law cannot abrogate, suspend, nor change a Cognitive Law or Natural Law. Nor is it possible for a Cognitive Law or Natural Law to abrogate, suspend or change a Divine Law. 16 All valid Positive Law is by Statutes within the limits of the established authority of the legislative body of the greater body politic. A legislative body cannot issue valid law which exceeds its mandate or jurisdiction. 17 An Act or Statute can only apply to the limits of jurisdiction of the properly constituted body that issued it. Therefore a legislative body of a lesser entity cannot legally or lawfully abrogate the laws of the higher estate that first created its franchise. 18 A Positive Law is established and takes force when it is promulgated. 19 The Second Law of Yapa is Positive Law. 20 Any law that is against such truth cannot be law.

C. 7 - Ecclesiastical Law

1 This be Ecclesiastical Law: 2 Ecclesiastical Law is the body of statutes and ordinances of an ecclesiastical entity issued by proper authority for the moderation of a religious organisation and its members. 3 As Ecclesiastical Law ultimately refers to rules created by men and women, not natural or divine, all valid Ecclesiastical Law may be said to be Positive Law and derived from Positive Law. 4 Ecclesiastical Law may not abrogate, change, suspend any Cognitive Law, Natural Law or Divine Law. 5 There exists no such force, concept or manifestation under Divine Law, Natural Law or Cognitive Law known as unholy. All forms of existence are sacred to some degree. 6 There exists no such force, concept or manifestation under Divine Law, Natural Law or Cognitive Law known as original sin or hereditary spiritual impairment or inherited debt. Any rule, ritual, claim, or ordinance based on such falsity is automatically reprobate, to be suppressed having no force or effect of law. 7 There exists no such force, concept or manifestation under Divine Law, Natural Law or Cognitive Law whereby a spirit or mind can be sold, or ceded, or claimed, or salvaged, or lost or abandoned. Any rule, ritual, claim, or ordinance based on such falsity is automatically reprobate, to be suppressed having no force or effect of law. 8 There exists no such force, concept, permission or manifestation under Divine Law, Natural Law or Cognitive Law whereby the living flesh of a higher order being may be treated as property that can be sold, or ceded, or claimed, or salvaged, or lost or abandoned for the purpose of slavery in any form or kind. Any rule, ritual, claim, or ordinance based on such

falsity is automatically reprobate, to be suppressed having no force or effect of law. 9 There exists no such force, concept or manifestation under Divine Law, Natural Law or Cognitive Law that permits living beings such as men and women to be treated as already dead, or in some form of purgatory, or underworld or hell or "mundi". Any rule, ritual, claim, or ordinance based on such falsity is automatically reprobate, to be suppressed having no force or effect of law. 10 There exists no such force, concept or manifestation under Divine Law, Natural Law or Cognitive Law that permits commerce and trade to be considered a transgression or sacrilege and therefore a crime. Any rule, ritual, claim, or ordinance based on such falsity is automatically reprobate, to be suppressed having no force or effect of law. 11 To the extent that Ecclesiastical Law is in accord with Natural Law, Cognitive Law and Divine Law, then such law may be said to be in agreement with law. To the extent that Ecclesiastical Law is not in accord with Natural Law, Cognitive Law and Divine Law, then such rules may be said to be in conflict with law. 12 Any law that is against such truth cannot be law.

C. 8 - Bioethics Law

1 This be Bioethics Law: 2 Bioethics Law is the body of statutes and ordinances of an ecclesiastical, sovereign or political entity issued by proper authority for the moderation of all forms of life, health, welfare, therapies, biotechnology, genetics and well being. 3 As Bioethics Law ultimately refers to rules created by men and women, not natural or divine, all valid Bioethics Law may be said to be Positive Law and derived from Positive Law. 4 As demonstrated by the laws of the Divine Creator and by virtue of reason and common sense, everything in the universe is made from the same fundamental building blocks of matter. Therefore, everything in the Universe may be described as having life to some degree. 5 In the case of Hydro-Carbon life, self-awareness is recognised as a trait possessed by all vertebrate animals to some degree. In the case of non-hydro carbon life, self-awareness is recognised as a trait possessed by only advanced autonomous neural computers. 6 Hydro-Carbon Life is recognised as the universal process of molecular evolution in a molecular atmosphere conducive for more complex molecular shapes leading to cellular life. As is demonstrated by the Divine Creator through the Natural Law, wherever the right conditions exist in the universe, other Hydro-Carbon life will exist. 7 Men and women are forbidden to claim ownership as property any physical element of animal life as such a false claim directly contradicts the obligations of their office as stewards of all life on Earth. Any law that falsely permits claims of ownership of genetic material is automatically rendered unnatural and inferior law by such gross error in permitting patently false law to be rendered in the first instance. 8 By the force of Natural law all life possesses its own unique genetic blueprint. A species blueprint that has not been artificially altered by man in any way is called an original form genome. A species genome that

has undergone major genetic modifications is a genetically modified species and not of the original form. 9 As custodians of all life upon the planet Earth by virtue of such office and obligations, all men and women have a duty to see that the original forms of all species genome are preserved in some way from future deliberate, accidental or evolutionary genetic modification. 10 As a result of the way cells regenerate, all species have a natural life expectancy. The natural life expectancy of the species Homo Sapien depends largely on the conditions of birth, existence of genetic defects, predisposition to certain diseases and life. However, it is not unreasonable to consider that the life expectancy of men and women during the 21st century might one day be 120 years or greater. 11 To die is a natural part of cellular life. While to extend the quality of life is a positive aspiration it should never be at the expense of the natural life experience of men and women. In any case, the right to chart the course of ones life remains totally within the claim by a man or woman demonstrating sound mind, with their wishes respected and to be carried out accordingly. 12 Homo Sapien are born naturally through the process of placental development over a period of approximately 300 days for a fully formed infant man or woman. Placental development is unique to other forms of development formation in that it actively requires a species to recreate the genetic evolution and history leading to the species by undergoing a period of actual existence of the 1st and simplest life until the final unique form of the species. 13 For the development of Homo Sapien, this placental development experience means 1 day of existence as mono cellular life, 1 day of life as the simplest multi-cellular life, then 10 days of life as a parasitic culture, 14 days of life as simple species life, then 14 days of life as a simple prototype mammal, then 14 days of life as a prototype primate and finally from around day 55 approximately 245 days as a developing Homo Sapien infant specie. 14 While a fetus of a child is not yet born until birth, there is no question that scientifically, legally and morally from day 55 to 60 onwards that the life-form within a mothers womb is Homo Sapien, therefore any death of the fetus from day 55 to 60 onwards is the death of a Homo Sapien- an unborn man or woman. 15 Any law that seeks to arbitrarily mandate that life of a Homo Sapien begins from day 1 of conception, or conversely does not recognise the indisputable fact that from day 55 to 60 onwards, the fetus is clearly an unborn man or woman is automatically rendered inferior and contrary to natural law. 16 All men and women are bestowed by our Divine Creator, also known as Unique Collective Awareness, Fixed and Irrevocable Title over their body, mind and spirit subject to Divine Law and that no force may lawfully abrogate any of these Rights, with or without our Consent. 17 Every man and woman is granted at birth Fixed and Irrevocable Title over their body therefore also their face and voice. 18 Any facsimile whether physical, digital in any form of image of face, body or voice remains a permanent extension of a man or woman's Fixed and

Irrevocable Title, therefore the property of that particular man or woman regardless of whether they commissioned the reproduction or not. 19 Unless consent is provided to make a recording, the recording of a face, body or voice of a man or woman contravenes their natural property rights and therefore is equivalent to property theft. Even when a man or woman consents to a recording, such an action in no way cedes ownership, merely the right to use those recordings in the manner agreed. 20 Regardless of whether an animal is kept for the ultimate purpose of having it killed and using its flesh for food, the life of every animal should be respected and handled with dignity. This is because an obligation of office bestowed upon all men and women as custodians of all animal Life on Earth and the obligation above all to be good and kind caretakers of all animals. 21 No animal should be kept in semi-permanent or permanent confinement and such barbaric conditions that it is unable to move itself freely and is deprived of basic dignity. Battery farms and factories that show no compassion towards the life of animals should not be permitted to continue in such models. 22 No animal should be subject to torture or prolonged agonising death, no matter what type of animal it is. Cruelty to any kind of life is without respect for life on Earth and life in general. No justification exists, no matter what the scientific purpose or claimed outcome that animals are subject to torture and prolonged pain. 23 As custodians over all life on Earth, no man or woman may rightfully claim a living animal that dreams as their property. While animals may be kept, tendered and even slaughtered for food, it is against natural law and the obligations of sovereign office to claim ownership of property that is ultimately the possession of the Divine Creator. 24 Any law that claims to permit ownership of animals that dream as property are in direct violation of the natural laws of the universe and the sovereign covenant between the Divine creator and every man and woman and therefore are from the beginning null and void, whether superior remedy has been presented or not. 25 Natural Foods are any natural substance born or grown on the land or from the sea, free from artificial genetic mutation and synthetic material, which contains a portion of the necessary amino acids, sugars, proteins and fluids required for normal healthy body function for a living man or woman. 26 Any law that seeks to restrict the use of natural foods in order to promote unnatural foods automatically is itself an unnatural law. When such unnatural laws are used to promote a commercial advantage for manufacturers of unnatural food products over natural food products, such laws are themselves immoral, unlawful and must be treated as nothing more than an organised criminal conspiracy. 27 Natural Drugs are any natural substance born or grown on the land or from the sea, free from artificial genetic mutation, which when ingested, injected or inhaled causes a physiological change in the body to some degree for a living man or woman. As all food when ingested causes extensive physiological changes in the body, especially sugar, all food can also be classed as drugs. 28 Natural Drugs that provide a degree of relief of pain or enhanced feeling of well being may be further classed as narcotic. Such Naturally grown drugs have been a feature of the lives of men and women in civilised society for thousands of years without dispute. 29 By right of natural law and common sense, all naturally grown or born food and drugs are created free, without debt or bond. This is in recognition to the indisputable fact that such naturally born substances and forms of life existed prior to the emergence of civilisation and if left unattended, many such substances and life forms grow and evolve of their own accord. 30 Any law that denies the right that naturally grown or born food and drugs are born or grown free defies natural law and therefore is automatically rendered inferior and in error. Any such remedy by law that properly represents natural law concerning natural food and drugs shall have precedence on inferior law, regardless of the false claims of such inferior and erroneous laws. 31 It is considered an immoral act and against nature that animals listed as endangered or protected are killed for food or sport. No counter claim that such acts represent science or cultural tradition shall prevail. 32 A man or woman has by right of natural law the right to grow natural food or drugs for free. This is in recognition of two indisputable facts that firstly such naturally born substances and forms of life have existed for thousands of years and secondly that all naturally grown food and drugs are born free and unencumbered of debt, bond or other obligation. 33 Any law that is against such truth cannot be law.

C. 9 - Sovereign Law

1 This be Sovereign Law: 2 A sovereign is a person defined by the will of a body politic as its supreme and highest fiduciary over an estate as its general executor and the underlying trust as its trustor. 3 Sovereign Law is the body of statutes and ordinances of an ecclesiastical or political entity issued by proper authority for the moderation of trusts and estates by sovereigns also known as General Executor(s). 4 By definition a sovereign requires the existence of some constituting document as the will of the body politic, the existence of the body politic, the existence of some property claimed as the rightful possession of the body politic, a body of laws being the laws derived from the constituting document and two or more members of the body politic. 5 By the very definition and meaning of Sovereign, a person appointed to such high office by sacred oath is obligated to three (3) ancient and primary tasks being Protect the Realm, Protect the Law and Protect and Serve the People. 6 To Protect and Defend the Claim of the Realm is the first obligation of the Sovereign as a legally defined entity possessing its own personality and rights. 7 To Protect and Defend the Law of the Realm is the second obligation of the Sovereign to ensure Rule of Law, Justice and Equality prevail. 8 To Protect, Defend and Serve the People (Subjects) of the Realm is the third sacred obligation of the Sovereign. 9 A Sovereign without constitutionally claimed authority

cannot be known as sovereign. 10 A Sovereign that does not possess a claimed realm (country) and a willingness to defend such a claim, is not sovereign. 11 A Sovereign that ceases to defend the law of the realm (country), abdicates authority to those willing to do so in absence of such competence. 12 A Sovereign that ceases to serve and defend the people abdicates legitimacy to those willing to do so. 13 As the highest fiduciary, no other person may claim highest jurisdiction over the same particular estate or underlying trust. 14 As a sovereign must be invested into such sacred office as a fiduciary, the office of sovereign can never be occupied or held by an agent. Therefore, neither a company or corporation may ecclesiastically, lawfully, legally or morally act in the capacity of a sovereign power. 15 By definition, a corporation or company presuming the claimed authority of the body politic possesses no sovereign power. 16 By definition, any corporation or company that seeks to act in the capacity of sovereign deliberately and willingly usurps the will of the body politic as criminals and traitors. 17 By definition, it is the legal, lawful, moral and ecclesiastical possession of a valid claim that forms the basis of an estate to which a sovereign as general executor may be appointed, not necessarily the possession of the property itself. Therefore, the absence of possessing any physical terrain is immaterial to the legitimacy of a claim of sovereignty. 18 As the legitimacy of a claim to possession of land is based upon the sacred and moral basis of such claim, the seizure by force of any property has no legal, moral or lawful effect on the rights of sovereign claim. 19 By definition, the mind of all men and women is Absolute Sovereign over their body through a True Trust granted through Divine Right of Use by Divine Trust. Therefore, no person, entity, spirit or force may abrogate, nor interpose themselves into or above such a sacred and inviolable covenant. 20 As irrevocable rights, the sovereignty of all lands granted to the original peoples of the land known as Australia cannot be ceded, sold, lost, abdicated, seized, surrendered, enclosed, partitioned, annexed, stolen or conveyed away from the legitimate body politic, estates and trusts of the original peoples. 21 Any claimed law, claim, edict, covenant, treaty, agreement, contract or instrument that claims some, part or all of the irrevocable and sovereign rights over all lands granted to the original peoples of the land known as Australia have been ceded, sold, seized, surrendered, enclosed, partitioned, annexed, stolen or conveyed away is automatically null and void from the beginning without force or effect of law. 22 Any law that is against such truth cannot be law.

C. 10 - Trust Law

1 This be Trust Law: 2 A Trust is a fictional Form of Relations and Agreement whereby certain Form, Rights and Obligations are lawfully conveyed to the administrative control of one or more fiduciary Persons for the benefit of one or more others. 3 The first key element of every valid and legitimate Trust is the sacred, formal and obligatory bond between the owner of the Property conveyed

and those entrusted to administer the terms of its use exemplified by the Intention of the Trust. A trust does not exist without clear Intention of conveyance. 4 The second key element of every valid and legitimate Trust is the sacred, formal and obligatory bond between those entrusted to administer its terms and those granted the beneficial use of the Property conveyed exemplified by the Purpose of Trust. A trust does not exist without clear Purpose. 5 All valid Trusts are considered sacred of the highest order on the presumption that all property is ultimately owned by the Divine Creator. To breach solemn trust is considered one of the gravest transgressions of Positive Law. 6 As Trusts, their formation and administration is considered sacred of the highest order, only those who have undertaken solemn oaths of service are entitled to properly administer them. These persons are called Fiduciary. 7 A Trust exists according to the terms of its formation in accord with its declared Intention and Purpose. When a Trust has fulfilled its Purpose, it automatically dissolves as a legitimate legal entity, whether or not those who previously administered it have agreed or not. 8 As valid and legitimate Trusts are considered sacred of the highest order, those who administer such Trusts as fiduciaries are expected to perform to the highest standard, in good faith, without prejudice and without conflict of interest. This standard is called Clean Hands. 9 Under the foundation of Trust Law, a fiduciary who fails to act with Clean Hands automatically ceases to be a legitimate fiduciary from the moment they failed in their duties, not the moment they were exposed, or called to give account or confessed their transgressions. 10 As valid and legitimate Trusts are considered sacred of the highest order, once formed, such valid and legitimate Trusts are considered unbreakable, whether or not the property related to them has been seized, stolen, damaged, enclosed, partitioned, surrendered, sold or unlawfully conveyed. 11 The highest form of Trust is a Divine Trust, also involving the highest form of rights of ownership. A Divine Trust is purely spiritual and divinely supernatural, formed in accord with the sacred Covenant *Pactum De Singularis Caelum* by the Divine Creator into which the form of Divine Spirit, Energy and Rights are conveyed. Therefore, a Divine Trust is the only possible type of Trust that can hold actual Form, rather than just the Rights of Use of Form (Property). 12 A Living Trust, also called an "Inter Vivos" Trust, involves the second highest form of rights of ownership. It is distinct from a Divine Trust or a Deceased (Testamentary) Trust that typically exists for a term of the lifetime of the Person(s) or Juridic Person(s) who are the beneficiaries. There are only four (4) valid forms of Living Trusts: True, Superior, Temporary and Inferior. 13 The second highest form of Trust also involving the second highest form of rights of ownership is a True Trust, being the highest form of Living Trust. A True Trust is formed in accord with the sacred Covenant *Pactum De Singularis Caelum* and the pre-existence of a Divine Trust in the lawful conveyance from the Divine Trust into the True Trust, the Divine

Rights of Use known as Divinity, being the highest possible form of any kind of Property. 14 The third highest form of any type of Trust is a Superior Trust, being the second highest form of Living Trust formed in accord with the Covenant *Pactum De Singularis Caelum* and the pre- existence of a True Trust in the lawful conveyance into the Superior Trust of Property, in the form of Realty being the highest form of Rights of Use of Object and Concepts by Divine Right, also known as Divinity. 15 A Temporary Trust is the third highest form of Living Trust involving the temporary conveyance of property from one (1) Superior Trust to another. 16 The lowest form of Living Trust possessing the lowest form of rights of ownership is called an Inferior Trust, also known as an Inferior Roman Trust, or simply Roman Trust. An Inferior Trust is any Living Trust formed by inferior Roman Law, claims and statutes. 17 A Deceased Trust, also known as a Testamentary Trust, also known as a Deceased Estate and simply a State, is the lowest form of Trust and the lowest form of rights of ownership of any possible form of Trust. Deceased Trusts are exclusively an invention of inferior Roman law, whereby property is conveyed into a Testamentary Trust upon the death of the testator. Inferior Roman law has defined a hybrid Deceased Trust called a Cestui Que Vie Trust which uses false and extraordinarily illogical presumptions to create Deceased Estates for the living on the presumption they are "dead" or lost or "abandoned to the sea". 18 Any claim that an Inferior Roman Trust possesses superior standing and rights of ownership compared to a Superior Trust, or True Trust, is an absurdity against Divine Law, Natural Law and Positive Law and therefore, is null and void from the beginning, including any associated covenants, deeds and agreements concerning property rights and lesser trusts. 19 The First Law of Yapa formed the first valid and legitimate Trusts of the people of the lands known as Australia more than 70,000 years ago. 20 The Second Law of Yapa formed the second valid and legitimate Trusts of the people of the lands known as Australia more than 45,000 years ago. 21 As Yapa has never been extinguished, nor have the Trusts of First Law and Trusts of Second Law been dissolved, all valid and legitimate trusts operating on the lands known as Australia are derived from Yapa. 22 Any law that is against such truth cannot be law.

C. 11 - Estate Law

1 This be Estate Law: 2 An Estate is a fictional form where certain property and rights in use, conveyance or dispute may be placed into a temporary trust and then a derivative of such assets known as an "estate" may be created and granted under title for use in commerce. 3 Two primary types of Estates exist being Superior and Inferior. Superior Estates concerns land and property granted in accord with the Covenant *Pactum De Singularis Caelum* and the absolute rights and uses granted from the Divine Creator through Divine Trusts into True Trusts and into Superior Trusts. Inferior Estates concern all Roman and Western legal constructs in law that by definition are without

legitimate land claims. 4 The concept of Inferior Estates were first invented under King Henry VIII of England as an legal argument to his seizure of property and rights from the Catholic Church. The creation of Estates was used to argue for all such "real" property or "land" being all the soil, all the people, all the "fruits of the land" and improvements of the land being placed into temporary trusts known as "Cestui Que Vie" Trusts until such time as the dispute or conflict ended, or a new Cestui Que Vie Trust was required to be created initially to a maximum 70 years and later to a limit of 99 years. Once corporations were created in greater frequency, the lengths of such temporary trusts were extended to much greater years. 5 Since the time of Henry VIII, all property seized was recorded into specific types of "rolls" with such records extracted and provided as certificates of title to nobles, merchants and people of the kingdom as "title" as a form of "derivative" and proof of existence of an estate in real property. 6 As the "rules" established from the time of King Henry VIII forbid the touching of the underlying property and trust in dispute, the possessor of title of the estate could hypothecate the implied value of the underlying property and then trade from units of that value created into a further derivative called a "fund" whereby accounts for the balancing of inbound demands or liabilities could be offset by outbound promissory notes or assets against units of the fund. 7 Any subsequent derivative instrument such as an annuity or other derivatives listed as assets not reflecting real estate or "land" were then to be treated as personal property or "asset backed securities" of the fund of the estate. 8 As every Estate requires the existence of a Trust prior to its existence, an Estate can never hold Real Property (Land). Real Estate implies merely first right of use within the constraints of the Estate, whereas Real Property implies the first right of use of a physical object or concept above all other claims. 9 One of the most detailed areas of the perpetuation of disputed property under Inferior Estates is in the area of inherited property. Hence, a Deceased Estate is the collective assets and liabilities of one or more deceased persons known as a Testator(s), endowed to one or more Heir(s), with certain Benefits accorded to one or more Beneficiaries and administered by Executors or court appointed Administrators acting as Executors. 10 The granting of Benefits to Beneficiaries is at the discretion of the Executors, also called Executives in accord with the terms of the Deed and Will of the Estate. A Beneficiary of an Estate may be a Person or if unknown, lost, a minor or abandoned a particular kind of Trust known as Cestui Que (Vie) Trust. 11 While a Public Trustee within the Roman System may be granted from time to time the position of Executor of a Trust belonging to the Inferior Estate of a Legal Person, by the very definition of Estate no agent, principal, trustee or entity may presume to claim the role of General Executor of the Estate of the Legal Person except the flesh, mind and spirit of the being for whom the Estate was first created. 12 When a man or woman acts as a trustee of one or more Trusts associated with an Inferior Estate of their Legal Person, the office of General Executor of the Estate is therefore vacant. However, when a man or woman demonstrating competence, wisdom, humility and duty gives public notice of their occupying the office of general executor of the estate of their Legal Person, no other trustee, public servant, agent or entity may usurp their authority concerning the estate. 13 As Yapa has never been extinguished, nor have the Trusts of First Law and Trusts of Second Law been dissolved, all valid and legitimate Estates operating on the lands known as Australia are derived from Yapa and are Superior Estates. 14 Any law that is against such truth cannot be law.

C. 12 - Company Law

1 This be Company Law: 2 A Company defines a form of society of members sharing some common "bond" defined by some formal instrument of self-rule. In the 16th Century, a second type of "company" was added being a corporate body having legal personality according to a constitution. In the 17th Century, a third type of "company" was added being a trust company formed by a deed in accordance to statute of law. 3 A Corporation, also referred to as a "company" is a 17th Century ecclesiastical and legal term meaning a corporate body possessing an instrument of incorporation and rules of authority and having legal personality according to one (1) or more statutes of a state or estate. A Corporation is one (1) of three (3) types of companies, the other two (2) being a Society and a form of Statutory Trust. 4 By definition, a Corporation is an association of one (1) or more persons that has undergone the ritual of incorporation. 5 There are essentially two (2) types of Corporations, distinguished primarily by their instrument and rules of incorporation being Chartered Corporations and Registered or Recognised Corporations. 6 Chartered Corporations are Corporations incorporated through the granting of some exclusive rights and privileges through charter or private act, often perpetual and validated by one (1) or more public or private acts of a legislative body of a sovereign estate. 7 Registered or Recognised Corporations are Corporations incorporated through the recognition of their existence, acceptance of certain rights and independence of rule by some constitution through treaty or registration. 8 By definition and logic, a Corporation cannot have greater power than the Corporation or Estate that formed it. 9 As a Company or Corporation formed from an Inferior Estate is by definition inferior to any Company formed from a Superior Estate, no Inferior Company can have powers greater than a Company formed from a Superior Estates. 10 As Yapa has never been extinguished, nor have the Trusts of First Law and Trusts of Second Law been dissolved, all valid and legitimate Companies operating on the lands known as Australia are derived from Yapa and Superior Estates. 11 Any law that is against such truth cannot be law.

C. 13 - Monetary Law

1 This be Monetary Law: 2 Money, or Currency is a formal system based on some standard unit of measurement, a store of value and a medium of payment and exchange. Money is anything that is generally accepted in exchange as payment for Goods according to some estimated value. 3 While the key function of money is to act as a medium of exchange, when money is formalised to be recognised as a store of value, a unit of account and method of payment according to certain rules, then it may be regarded then as Currency. 4 All currencies and therefore money may be defined into two (2) types according to the method of underwriting the value of the money: Commodity and Property. 5 Commodity Currency is the simplest form of currency whereby the money itself is the underwriting and carrier of value. The most common examples of commodity currency are gold and silver coins, now rarely minted in favour of debased metal coins of less intrinsic value. 6 Property Currency is any currency that uses Rights of Property by claim, lien and other mechanisms as the method of underwriting. All Property Currency is based upon the rules of Negotiable Instruments and the associated concept of Temporary Trusts in which to convey the Property. 7 All Notes, also known as Bank Notes and Bills are by definition fungible Negotiable Instruments, therefore Property Currency based upon one or more classes of Property conveyed into Temporary Trusts as its store of value. A Bank may choose to issue one Bank Note against one Temporary Trust for one Trust Corpus of Property, or may choose to issue multiple Bank Notes against a Temporary Trust to the total value of the Trust Corpus. 8 As Yapa has never been extinguished, nor have the Trusts of First Law and Trusts of Second Law been dissolved, all valid Currency and legitimate Money operating on the lands known as Australia are derived from Yapa and are Superior Estates. 9 No private company, nor private estate, nor private entity is permitted to issue Currency or Money for or on behalf of Australia. All Currency must be public currency. 10 Once created, any unit of Currency issued and underwritten by the Assets of Yapa cannot be destroyed, or fractionalised. 11 While fees for service are permitted, any unit of Currency issued and underwritten by the Assets of Yapa cannot be subject to any form of interest calculation, whereby units of currency are created or destroyed purely from mathematical equation. 12 Any law that is against such truth cannot be law.

C. 14 - Legislative Law

1 This be Legislative Law: 2 Legislative Law is the body of laws or "acts" passed, amended or repealed by an assembly possessing the authority and personality of a body politic. By definition, Legislative Law can only extend by jurisdiction to those members of the body politic. 3 An Act, is a written law, also known as a Statute or "statutory law", that is formally ordained and approved by a Juridic Person and a Superior Authority through a process known as a "Legislative Act". 4 Acts are either

public or private: (i) Public Acts, also called "general acts" or general statutes or statues at large are those which relate to the community generally or establish a universal rule for the governance of the whole body politic; and (ii) Private Acts, also known as "special acts" relate either to a particular person (personal acts) or particular places (local acts) or which operate only upon specific individuals or their private concerns. 5 An Act or Statute can only apply to the limits of jurisdiction of the Juridic Person that issued it. Therefore a legislative body of a corporation cannot legally or lawfully abrogate the laws of the higher estate that first created its franchise. 6 An Act and Statute must reflect the proper form and procedures prescribed by law and custom relating to the Parliamentary process of enacting law. 7 A valid Act of Law exists in form as a precise, brief and clear expression of the intention of Parliament in reflecting the needs and mandate of the people. Therefore, the more complex and long worded an act, or the less clear its intention, the greater chance part or all of it may be repealed by judicial review if challenged. 8 A proposed new Act and Statute must concern itself with one (1) main cause whereby its clauses and divisions reflect a consistent intention. A valid Act may not contain multiple causes or riders or contingencies to it. 9 Acts and Statutes that possess penalties and punishments must be construed strictly. 10 One (1) part of a new Act and Statute must be able to be so construed by another part of an existing Act, that the new Act may be considered a seamless addition to the wholly body of law. 11 A part or whole new Act and Statute that is totally repugnant to the existing body of law is automatically void, even if approved and assented. 12 Where the existing body of law and a new Act or Statute differ, the existing body of law has precedence, unless the new Act presents a considered, superior and reasoned argument to the contrary. 13 If an Act and Statute that repeals another, is itself repealed afterwards, the first Act and Stature is hereby revived without any formal words for that purpose. 14 Acts derogatory from the power of subsequent parliaments cannot be binding. 15 Acts and Statutes that seek to grant or exclude certain rights, property or uses in perpetuity, without consideration for expiry are null and void from the beginning. 16 Acts that are impossible to be performed are of no validity. 17 As the Parliament of the United Kingdom of Great Britain and Ireland formed in 1801 is a corporate franchise created by the authority of the Parliament of the united kingdom of Great Britain and the (now dissolved) Parliament of Ireland, it possesses less authority and jurisdiction than the body that created it. Therefore, all Acts of Law passed by the Parliament of the United Kingdom since 1801 have no legal or lawful effect over the citizens of Great Britain and only apply to employees of the Bank of England as Citizens of the United Kingdom Of Great Britain And Northern Ireland. 18 Any law that is against such truth cannot be law.

C. 15 - Civil Law

1 This be Civil Law: 2 Civil Law is a codified non-criminal legal system

introduced first in England in the late 17th Century and then in Europe by the 19th Century pertaining to the identity, rights, responsibilities, obligations and agreements between persons, particularly persons as citizens. 3 The claim that Civil Law existed from the time of the Roman Empire is false as the work published in 1583 as Corpus Iuris Civilis is a complete and utter fraud, therefore null and void from the beginning. 4 The primary purpose of Civil Law is to standardise the treatment of procedures and disputes concerning persons and their identity, rights, responsibilities, obligations and agreements without requiring judicial precedents, decisional law or case law. 5 Civil law by definition has jurisdiction over legal persons but cannot have jurisdiction over superior persons defined by Yapa. 6 Any law that is against such truth cannot be law.

C. 16 - Judicial Law

1 This be Judicial Law: 2 Judicial Law are the statutes, codes, policies and procedures guiding the rights, obligations, responsibilities, duties, appointment, management, conduct and oversight of all judicial officials and their agents. 3 Any official or agent or person performing any action for and on behalf of the judicial system including (but not limited to) the courts, justice system, clerks, trustees, police, bailiffs, sheriffs, collections, security, corrections is subject to Judicial Law. 4 Any one who occupies for any length of time the position of judge, or magistrate or arbitrator or administrator is required under oath, to pledge their recognition and obedience to the law of Yapa. 5 Any one who occupies for any length of time the position of judge, or magistrate or arbitrator or administrator who refuses to give an oath to Yapa and to adjudicate a matter in good faith, with clean hands and without prejudice is an impostor and a fraud. 6 No one may occupy the position of judge, or magistrate or arbitrator or administrator or clerk if they have any direct or indirect financial interest in the matter at hand. To fail to disclose such financial interest is an act of deliberate fraud and injury against justice. 7 Any law that is against such truth cannot be law.

C. 17 - Cultural Law

1 This be Cultural Law: 2 Cultural Law are the laws governing the creation, registration, recognition, preservation, protection and custody of the cultural legacy and sacred objects of the people. 3 All tribes and nations under Yapa are required to have their own unique Register of Cultural Objects that no object may be granted, given, displayed, bought, sold, moved unless it be duly registered and possess a unique record of its provenance and terms of use. 4 No one other than the nation or tribe of origin may claim a Cultural Object under Yapa, nor may seek to register it by their own means. 5 No one may own a Cultural Object. All Cultural Objects are by custody only. Anyone who claims ownership of a Cultural Object automatically ceases to have any rights to hold it. 6 Anyone possessing a Cultural Object of the people that is not duly registered in a

valid Register of Cultural Objects possesses no rights of custodianship and therefore no right to hold it, sell it or use it. 7 No art, sound, icon, imagery depicting a matter of traditional culture may be created unless it is duly registered in a Register of Cultural Objects having been granted permission by one or more duly authorised tribes or nations. 8 No Cultural Object may be bought, sold, leased, granted, given or conveyed unless it is duly registered on a valid Register of Cultural Objects. 9 Any law that is against such truth cannot be law.

C. 18 - Community Law

1 This be Community Law: 2 Any one physically born upon the land known as Australia belongs to the great spirit of Australia and is automatically part of the community of Yapa, whether a tribe or nation officially recognises such fact. 3 It is the obligation and solemn sacred duty of each tribe and nation to recognise the inherit rights of community recognition for all people physically born upon the land known as Australia. 4 A community, subject to its proper laws, may choose to adopt a man or woman to their community, providing they choose to live within the jurisdiction of the community. 5 No one who is a valid member of a community may be prejudiced on the basis of their skin colour, length of ancestral connection to the land, race of origin or gender. 6 Any law that is against such truth cannot be law.

C. 19 - International Law

1 This be International Law: 2 Valid Communities under Yapa may enter into agreements with other communities in accordance to International Law and the laws of Yapa. 3 No treaty, agreement, pledge, contract, promise, grant, gift or conveyance is valid if it effectively seeks to derogate or abrogate any part of the rights, powers, authorities and validity of Yapa. 4 Any treaty, agreement, pledge, contract, promise, grant, gift or conveyance that claims to derogate or abrogate any part of the rights, powers, authorities and validity of Yapa is automatically null and void from the beginning having no effective force of law. 5 Any law that is against such truth cannot be law.

Book 11
One Law One People One Country

C. 1 - One Law One People One Country

1 There is, there was, there has only ever been One Law, 2 there has only ever been One People, 3 there has only be One Country. 4 There can be no honour of First People, 5 if there is no honour or recognition of First Law, 6 the Three unbroken Ages of Law of Yapa. 7 There can be no honour of One Country, 8 unless First Law and first People are recognised. 9 No one is above such Law. 10 No one of Community is excluded from such Law. 11 All are equal under the One Law. 12 Any law that is against such truth, cannot be law.

C.2 - People borne to Country borne to People

1 Any one borne to Country is borne to People, 2 is borne to tribe and Law. 3 People be not by colour, 4 People be not by race of ancestors, 5 People be not by city or non-city. 6 Any one who rejects the right of people borne to Country, 7 as true members of tribe and the people, 8 dishonours the Law, 9 and dishonours their ancestors, 10 and dishonours the spirits of Country, 11 and is an impostor with no rights, 12 to speak of law or culture. 13 Racism is not Law, it is against proper Law. 14 Racial purity is not Law, it is madness of mind. 15 For every one borne of Country, 16 has the right to know the tribe they be borne, 17 and the ancient names of the land, 18 and be welcomed to tribe by right ceremony. 19 Any law that is against such truth, cannot be law.

C.3 - First Law does not need Treaty but Lawful People

1 Yapa as First Law existed for many tens of thousands of years, 2 before the laws of Europe and European banks. 3 Yapa as First Law does not need the permission of such powers, 4 to be true and First Law of the Country of Australia. 5 Yapa as First Law of Australia has never ceased being first law, 6 nor can true rule of law be usurped by treaty, 7 or by trickery or by other deception, 8 or by any other morally repugnant means. 9 Any law that seeks to claim itself as superior, 10 by making or having made morally repugnant claims, 11 or sacrilegious or absurd claims, 12 disqualifies itself as legitimate law, 13 so long as such absurd or morally repugnant claims, 14 are permitted to be enforced or demanded. 15 First Peoples as First

Law do not need a treaty, 16 but such law that is younger and defective and full of error, 17 needs Yapa as First Law to make it proper law. 18 So long as lesser law refuses to recognise First Law, 19 such inferior law cannot be law. 20 Whenever the First Law of Yapa is denounced or denied, 21 no such place can be called a place of law. 22 No act of tyranny in the face of such truth can make a false act true. 23 Any law that is against such truth, cannot be law.

C.4 Every Community is a Tribal Nation

1 Every community of Country is a Tribal Nation of Australia, 2 borne to tribe and law, 3 under the highest Law of Yapa. 4 Any one who rejects the truth that every community of naturally born native inhabitants of Australia are a Tribal Nation, 5 dishonours the Law, 6 and dishonours their ancestors, 7 and dishonours the spirits of Country, 8 and is an impostor with no rights to speak of law or culture. 9 No part of Country, 10 no part of Australia is without a Tribal Nation. 11 Each Tribal Nation as community of Australia, 12 be an Original Tribal Nation, 13 and first nation and dominion and sovereignty above all others. 14 No claim of sovereignty or dominion or control or right of Country be higher than the members of an Original Tribal Nation of Australia. 15 The leaders of each Original Tribal Nation be the leaders elected by the naturally born native inhabitants as members of the community, 16 no matter what the colour of their skin, 17 or the ancestry of their parents or grandparents, 18 or their gender or religion. 19 Any traditional leader of a community recognised by form of government who rejects their sacred obligation to Law and Yapa, 20 and who refuses to help educate and support the life of an Original Tribal Nation, 21 loses any and all authority no matter their initiation or claim of power. 22 Any form of government that refuses to acknowledge each community of Country as an Original Tribal Nation, 23 disavows the true rule of law of Australia, 24 and declares itself to be without authority or right, 25 but a belligerent foreign occupying force that must be driven out from country. 26 Any community leader that denies their authority comes from the community, 27 and comes from the first law of community as Yapa, 28 declares themselves without proper power or authority, 29 and an impostor who must be expelled from community and the Original Tribal Nation.

C.5 - Sacred Trust of Each Tribal Nation

1 The rights and powers of every community of Country as an Original Tribal Nation, 2 are permanently vested in sacred trust as the rights and powers of naturally born native inhabitants of Australia, 3 whose rights cannot be seized or forfeited or suspended or surrendered by trickery or force. 4 Nor may such sacred and divine rights and powers be transferred, or disavowed, or alienated, or sold or given away to any body or association or person, except by lawful means of a union between all Original Tribal Nations. 5 Because all

the rights and powers of naturally born native inhabitants of each community of Australia are permanently vested and protected in sacred and irrevocable trust, 6 with the elected leaders of each community as trustees, 7 any claim of older trusts or higher trusts or greater trusts, 8 be null and void and without spiritual or moral or sovereign or lawful validity and legitimacy, 9 except for any trust formed by lawful means of a union between all Original Tribal Nations. 10 Any instruments, treaties, deeds, charters, covenants, promises, contracts of any kind that have existed or still exist, 11 upon any claim or assertion in defiance of the highest and superior rights and powers of each sacred trust of each and every Original Tribal Nation of Australia are hereby null and void, without spiritual or moral or sovereign or lawful validity and legitimacy. 12 Only instruments, treaties, deeds, charters, covenants, promises, contracts of any kind, 13 that recognise the rights and powers of members of each community as an Original Tribal Nation, 14 under the rule of law of Yapa, 15 be valid or legitimate instruments if they honour the laws of Ucadia. 16 Any transfer of wealth, capital, money, resources or other things of value that continue or have continued or will continue, 17 against the natural born rights of community members of Australia, 18 that impoverishes such members for the benefit of some foreign body or claimant, 19 in defiance of the true rule of law, 20 is and shall be a profoundly immoral, unlawful and sacrilegious act against any notion of rule of law. 21 Any person or office holder that defies the rule of law and commits a profoundly immoral act against a community of country, 22 as an Original Tribal Nation of Australia, 23 forfeits any right or claim of right of immunity or protection, 24 and shall be held responsible personally three times for each every such unlawful act in defiance of the existence and form of sacred trusts of Australia.

C.6 - Body Politic of each Tribal Nation

1 Each and every Original Tribal Nation of Australia, 2 be a sovereign body politic, 3 with its own laws and bylaws, 4 and its own executive and legislature, 5 with the present sacred Covenant as its first Governing Instrument of Formation and Constitution, 6 before members may decide by vote to form a separate constitution in accord with the present most sacred Covenant. 7 Each and every Original Tribal Nation of Australia as a body politic shall have the same rights as a natural person, 8 to engage and treaty with other persons, bodies and corporations, 9 and to bring suit or to have actions brought against it to the extent that sovereign immunity shall protect the essential sovereign integrity of each and every community of Australia. 10 The unit of account for each Original Tribal Nation of Australia shall be the Ucadia Moneta, 11 and any unit of currency that claims to be by authority of a government of Australia, or for the community of Australia shall first and foremost be derived from the accounts and funds of Ucadia Moneta and no other, in accord with the Ucadia Financial System. 12 No body

or bank or fund or agency shall have any right or claim to be a central bank for any Original Tribal Nation or group of Original Tribal Nations of Australia, 13 unless it be a body authorised under the Ucadia Financial System, 14 and no person or group of people or corporations may claim to be a central bank of Australia, 15 or any part of Australia, 16 as the sovereign right of communities of Australia to mint and manage money, 17 is a sacred right that cannot be seized, surrendered, alienated, sold, forfeited or abrogated in any way.

C.7 - Union of Original Nations of Australia

1 The unity of country and unity of Australia, 2 exists first and foremost through the Union of all Original Tribal Nations of Australia as one united body politic, 3 and the formation of a sacred united trust between all Original Tribal Nations of Australia, 4 and the lawful recognition and incorporation by charter of an executive and body politic and corporate to serve the interests of all Australians first and foremost, 5 rather than the interests of foreign bodies, potentates, powers or other persons. 6 The primary legislative organ of the Union of all Original Nations of Australia shall be the Council of Original Nations of Australia, also to be known simply as the (Original) Australian Council. 7 The primary executive corporate sole of the Union of all Original Nations of Australia shall be the President of the Council of Original Nations of Australia, 8 also known simply as the (Original) President of Australia. 9 The body politic and corporate formed underneath the authority and powers of the Council of Original Nations of Australia, 10 shall be known as the Commonwealth of Australia, 11 also known simply as the Government of Australia and the Australian Government. 12 The primary executive corporate sole of Commonwealth of Australia shall be the Prime Minister or President, is custom changes for naming. 13 The Governing Instrument of the Commonwealth of Australia shall first and foremost be the Law of Yapa and the laws of Ucadia, 14 and secondly those customary instruments and constitutions of claimed unity of Australia, 15 to the extent that they are neither morally repugnant or contradict the principles of true law, justice and due process as defined by Yapa and the laws of Ucadia. 16 All other claims of sovereignty, authority, union and validity shall be secondary to the Union of all Original Nations of Australia. 17 Where officials acting in the claimed capacity as the Commonwealth of Australia or Government of Australia refuse to recognise Yapa, 18 or refuse to recognise the Union of all Original Nations of Australia, 19 then all valid and legitimate spiritual, ecclesiastical, sovereign, moral, lawful and legitimate executive and legislative authority shall be vested solely with the Council of Original Nations of Australia, 20 who then shall have every right, power to call for aid and assistance in the defeat of any and all forces of occupation, oppression or tyranny upon the country of Australia. 21 However, if there exists officials acting in the claimed capacity as the Commonwealth of Australia or

Government of Australia that properly recognise the authority of Yapa and Ucadia, 22 then all sovereign, moral, lawful and legitimate executive and legislative authority shall be vested solely with the Government of Australia, 23 and the the Council of Original Nations of Australia shall hold reserve and emergency powers only, in the event of a coup or seizure of power in defiance of the laws of Yapa and Ucadia.

C.8 - State and Union of Original Nations of Australia

1 The Council of Original Nations of Australia and the present Governing Instrument, 2 recognise the permission of groups of Original Tribal Nations in forming smaller regional groups. 3 These smaller regional groups shall be called States or Territories, 4 and may be formed only upon a convention of Original Tribal Nations as a Union of Australia. 5 A small region of united Original Tribal Nations shall only be permitted to use names and boundaries determined by the union convention, 6 and in respect of customary traditions and names. 7 However, a regional body of Original Tribal Nations is not permitted to form treaty with any foreign body deriving its claim or authority from some foreign occupying force upon country. 8 Any body currently called a state or territory that refuses to acknowledge the higher authority of Yapa and the laws of Ucadia, 9 and instead seeks to maintain a claim of authority and power from a foreign sovereign or body, 10 shall then declare itself to be an occupying and oppressive force that cannot be given spiritual or moral or lawful legitimacy. 11 the Council of Original Nations of Australia shall have every right, power to call for aid and assistance, 12 in the defeat of any and all such forces of occupation, oppression or tyranny upon the country of Australia.

C.9 - Sacred Tribal Registers of Australia

1 All rights and property of Australia comes first from the laws of Yapa, 2 and the laws of Ucadia and the sacred tribal registers of Australia. 3 No right or claim to property or land or tenement or thing of value be valid or legitimate, 4 unless the register or roll recording such an entry be a valid and legitimate sacred tribal register of the Union of Original Nations of Australia. 5 Any register or roll that is not itself registered as a valid and legitimate tribal register of the Council of Original Nations of Australia, 6 shall have no spiritual, ecclesiastical, sovereign, moral, lawful or legitimate authority whatsoever, no matter how old or how well established. 7 The Council of Original Nations of Australia shall have a moral and spiritual obligation, 8 to ensure the safe protection and administration of property rights of the people of Australia, 9 and for existing registers to be recognised as valid and legitimate sacred tribal registers, providing such registers to not repudiate the moral obligations and needs of the communities and people of Australia. 10 Registers that openly repudiate common sense and moral obligation to the people and

communities of Australia mist be refused recognition, 11 and to be dissolved and removed at the earliest opportunity, 12 including the dissolution of those laws that made such registers and rolls repugnant and contrary to the laws of Yapa and the laws of Ucadia. 13 Above all it is better that a register be reformed and then recognised than banned and forced to be dissolved, given the disruption to the certainty of rights and property.

C.10 - Sacred Tribal Cultural Registers

1 All rights of use, benefit, sale and ownership of indigenous art, artefacts and cultural items of significance shall be subject to the Sacred Tribal Cultural Registers of Australia, 2 under the primary authority and control of the Council of Original Nations of Australia. 3 Only indigenous art, artefacts and cultural items duly registered in a valid and legitimate Sacred Tribal Cultural register are permitted to be held, displayed, owned or used. 4 Indigenous art, artefacts and cultural items not properly registered in a valid and legitimate Sacred Tribal Cultural register are not permitted to be held, displayed, owned, offered for sale or used. 5 The holding, displaying, selling of items claiming to be indigenous or indigenous cultural items of significance without a proper registration number, 6 shall represent one of most profoundly morally repugnant, wicked and sacrilegious crimes that a government, or agency, or officer, or body or institution or person may commit against country and the people of Australia.

C.11 - Sacred Tribal Land Registers

1 All rights of use, benefit and ownership of land or space shall be subject to the Sacred Land Registers of Australia, 2 under the primary authority and control of the Council of Original Nations of Australia. 3 No register or roll of land rights or usage shall be valid or legitimate unless the specific register is itself duly registered and recognised as a Sacred Tribal Land Register in accord with the present sacred laws of Yapa and laws of Ucadia. 4 A register that contradicts any of the following fundamental spiritual, sovereign and moral principles in relation to the people and communities of Australia is to be forbidden, suppressed and not permitted to be recognised as a valid or legitimate register whatsoever: 5 First, only Australians members of an Original Nation or an Australian company may own land or buildings or property. 6 Second, non-Australians being foreign bodies, sovereign powers, foreign citizens may not purchase or own land or buildings or property, 7 as such bodies or powers persons may only lease land or buildings or property from Australians. 8 If a register permits such foreign ownership then a sale or transfer of ownership must be completed on all such foreign owned property before such a register can be considered for legitimacy. 9 Third, primary property rights of Australian natural persons shall not exceed ninety-nine years and fifty-five years for an Australian company respectively. 10 Fourth, the lease of land or buildings or property by

foreign natural persons shall not exceed twenty five years and twelve years for a foreign body or company respectively.

C.12 - Sacred Tribal Mineral Registers

1 All rights of use, benefit and ownership of minerals and mining shall be subject to the Sacred Mineral Registers of Australia, 2 under the primary authority and control of the Council of Original Nations of Australia. 3 No register or roll of land rights or usage shall be valid or legitimate unless the specific register is itself duly registered and recognised as a Sacred Tribal Land Register in accord with the present sacred laws of Yapa and laws of Ucadia. 4 A register that contradicts any of the following fundamental spiritual, sovereign and moral principles in relation to the people and communities of Australia is to be forbidden, suppressed and not permitted to be recognised as a valid or legitimate register whatsoever: 5 First, only Australians members of an Original Nation or an Australian company may own mineral rights. 6 Second, non-Australians being foreign bodies, sovereign powers, foreign citizens may not own mineral rights, 7 as such bodies or powers persons may only lease mineral rights from Australians. 8 If a register permits such foreign ownership then a sale or transfer of ownership must be completed on all such foreign owned mineral rights before a register can be considered for legitimacy. 9 Third, the value of any mineral rights and applications assigned any land shall not exceed one tenth the value of the surface valuation of the land. 10 Fourth, the right of first claim for mineral rights and application shall always be vested in the primary Australian owner of the land. 11 Fifth, the total value of claims and mineral rights of a person or company shall not exceed three times the net asset value of the person or company prior to making such mineral claims and applications. 12 Sixth, excluding the primary owner of the land, a mineral claim or right shall be extinguished within three years if active building, investment, mining and extraction does not commence and continue for an accumulative period of not less than six months during the period.

C.13 - Sacred Tribal Water Registers

1 All rights of use, benefit and ownership of water shall be subject to the Sacred Land and Registers of Australia, 2 under the primary authority and control of the Council of Original Nations of Australia. 3 No register or roll of land rights or usage shall be valid or legitimate unless the specific register is itself duly registered and recognised as a Sacred Tribal Land Register in accord with the present sacred laws of Yapa and laws of Ucadia. 4 A register that contradicts any of the following fundamental spiritual, sovereign and moral principles in relation to the people and communities of Australia is to be forbidden, suppressed and not permitted to be recognised as a valid or legitimate register whatsoever: 5 First, only Australians members of an Original Nation or an Australian company may own water rights. 6

Second, non-Australians being foreign bodies, sovereign powers, foreign citizens may not own water rights, 7 as such bodies or powers persons may only lease water rights from Australians. 8 Third, the value of any water rights and applications assigned to any related land shall not exceed one tenth the value of the surface valuation of the land. 9 Fourth, the right of first claim for water rights and application shall always be vested in the primary Australian owner of the land related to the water rights. 10 Fifth, the claimant for purchase of water rights must live or operate its primary business within the catchment associated with the said water rights. 11 Sixth, the total value of claims and water rights of a person or company shall not exceed three times the net asset value of the person or company prior to making such water claims and applications. 12 Seventh, excluding the primary owner of the land, a mineral claim or right shall be extinguished within three years if utilisation of at least sixty five percent of such water rights does not commence and continue for an accumulative period of not less than six months.

C.14 – Courts and Enforcement of Rule of Law

1 True law is not morally repugnant. 2 True law is logical and sensible. 3 A true and valid and legitimate court is one that honours the Law of Yapa and Ucadia. 4 Any forum of law that does not honour or recognise or respect Yapa as first law cannot be a proper court of law, 5 but must be a sacrilegious and wicked and morally repugnant place of injury to the true rule of law. 6 A jurist or recorder or judge that seeks to usurp the rule of law, 7 by refusing to recognise the primary of Yapa and the laws of Ucadia, 8 declares himself an enemy of heaven, 9 and an enemy to all forms of spirit and the laws of the universe, 10 and belligerent threat to all forms of life of earth, 11 and an enemy of the people of Australia. 12 Such a person calls upon themselves the worst of woe and ill. 13 Yet such a person or persons must also be held to account. 14 Yapa is judged by no one. 15 Ucadia is judged by no one. 16 Any forum claiming to be a forum of law that denies such truth cannot be a proper court of law, 17 nor may any order, verdict or sentence stand as anything but a solemn and profound curse upon the makers of such false instruments. 18 Do not fear those who curse themselves and their brethren by wicked acts against the law. 19 Respect the true law. 20 Embrace Yapa, 21 as Yapa loves you. 22 Peace be upon you and all the communities of Country.

www.ingramcontent.com/pod-product-compliance
Lightning Source LLC
Chambersburg PA
CBHW080442170426
43195CB00017B/2865